ROUTLEDGE LIBRARY EDITIONS:
INDUSTRIAL RELATIONS

Volume 20

INDUSTRIAL RELATIONS IN THE MODERN STATE

INDUSTRIAL RELATIONS IN THE MODERN STATE

An Introductory Survey

R. KEITH KELSALL
AND
T. PLAUT

Routledge
Taylor & Francis Group

LONDON AND NEW YORK

First published in 1937 by Methuen & Co. Ltd.

This edition first published in 2025
by Routledge
4 Park Square, Milton Park, Abingdon, Oxon OX14 4RN

and by Routledge
605 Third Avenue, New York, NY 10158

Routledge is an imprint of the Taylor & Francis Group, an informa business

British Library Cataloguing in Publication Data
A catalogue record for this book is available from the British Library

ISBN: 978-1-032-81770-5 (Set)
ISBN: 978-1-032-81419-3 (Volume 20) (hbk)
ISBN: 978-1-032-81421-6 (Volume 20) (pbk)
ISBN: 978-1-003-49976-3 (Volume 20) (ebk)

DOI: 10.4324/9781003499763

Publisher's Note
The publisher has gone to great lengths to ensure the quality of this reprint but
points out that some imperfections in the original copies may be apparent.

Disclaimer
The publisher has made every effort to trace copyright holders and would
welcome correspondence from those they have been unable to trace.

INDUSTRIAL RELATIONS IN
THE MODERN STATE

AN INTRODUCTORY SURVEY

by

R. KEITH KELSALL, M.A.

ASSISTANT LECTURER IN ECONOMICS AT
UNIVERSITY COLLEGE, HULL

and

T. PLAUT, Dr. RER. POL.

FORMERLY PROFESSOR OF COMMERCE AT
THE UNIVERSITY OF HAMBURG, AND AT
UNIVERSITY COLLEGE, HULL

METHUEN & CO. LTD. LONDON
36 Essex Street Strand W.C.2

First published in 1937

PRINTED IN GREAT BRITAIN

CONTENTS

INTRODUCTION

ANY ONE who sets out to add to the already excessive number of books relating to industrial relations must be prepared to offer some excuse for his temerity. The excuse offered on this occasion is simply this; that there exists no up-to-date and brief introduction to the subject in English which compares the position in different countries; and that such a guide to those first approaching the study of labour problems is even more necessary now than formerly, because of a change which has come over their study in the last decade or so. We propose to devote this introduction to a discussion of the nature of that change.

When the Continental student of pre-war days embarked upon the study of social economics, the teaching he received related in the main to English methods of approaching labour questions; the special problems of his own country were regarded as of secondary importance. Of the four standard text-books the German student was expected to use, only one dealt specifically with his own country.[1] The reason for this state of affairs is obvious. England was the first country to experience an industrial revolution, and had done

---

[1] Lujo Brentano, *Die Arbeitergilden*, gives the history of trade unionism in England. v. Schulze-Gaevernitz, *Zum Socialen Frieden* deals with the development of social thought in England. v. Nostiz, *Der Aufstieg der Arbeiterklasse Englands* explains the development of labour legislation in England. Herkner, *Die Arbeiterfrage*, is a text-book of labour problems in which German labour problems take a prominent place.

most of the pioneer work in connexion with the social problems which such a revolution created or accentuated. It was therefore almost inevitable that Continental scholars should study the development of social policy in England. Probably most of those who studied England's methods believed that she was working on the right lines; socialist theorists did not, of course, subscribe to this view, but their direct influence on government policy was as yet small. There was a marked tendency to regard the trend of social policy in England as foreshadowing the lines of development in other countries.

With the striking changes in the political and economic framework of two states, Russia and Italy, in the post-war period, however, a change of attitude developed. The social policy of these states soon emerged from the merely experimental stage; and even before Germany ventured on large-scale experiments of her own, it had become obvious that the student of labour questions would have to take account of the new approach which the social policy of these states represented. England no longer sets the standard in this respect which other nations accept and strive, with varying degrees of success, to reach; you have instead a variety of possible standards, and some study of the principles underlying them is essential. Our main purpose, then, is to explain the newer methods of approach to labour problems and to compare them with the traditional attitude generally adopted before the War and still maintained in many liberal states. We use the term "liberal state", it should be explained, as meaning a capitalist state in which, in the economic sphere, it is the general principle (notwithstanding many exceptions) to allow the individual freedom of initiative; and in which, in the political sphere, some form of democratic parliamentary machinery is in effective operation. The United Kingdom, France, Germany before 1933, the Netherlands, Norway, Sweden, Switzerland and the U.S.A. are therefore regarded as liberal states.

Naturally, then, we are concerned with a comparison of principles rather than of details, and no attempt will be made to give a complete account of the labour policy and provisions of any state. It may be felt that we ought to give, at the outset, some account of the rival philosophies underlying the totalitarian and the liberal state. This we hardly feel qualified to do; but a quotation from C. E. M. Joad puts the matter, in our opinion, as clearly and concisely as it can be put.[1] "The issue raised is," he says, "one of ultimate values. There is first the question of the value which we place upon the State. There are those who, regarding the community as the ultimate source of virtue and value, conceive of it as delegating certain freedoms to individuals temporarily and for special purposes and under strict injunctions as to good behaviour; and there are those who, regarding individuality as the ultimate source of virtue and value, conceive of individuals as agreeing to delegate certain functions to the Government for purposes of convenience. . . . Is the State the source of such personality as I possess, or is it a device for carrying out certain purposes which I have in common with my neighbours?" It is against a background of this kind that the labour policies of different countries should, therefore, be examined to-day; and this is particularly necessary because though the provisions of two countries on some labour questions may look

[1] In the preface to Joseph Wood Krutch, *Was Europe a Success?* (1935).

similar, the spirit in which these provisions are applied may be totally different. It should be added that no conscious attempt to pass judgment on the desirability of one policy rather than another will be made in cases where any such attempt would entail criticism of the whole basis on which a state is organized and governed.

A list of books is given at the end of each chapter. These lists make no claim to be exhaustive, but are merely a selection of the available literature in English, with an occasional reference to works in another language; usually at least one of the books mentioned in each list, however, contains a bibliography. The provision of these book-lists represents, of course, an admission on our part that any one who is seriously interested in any particular aspect of the subject will want much fuller information than we are able to give him here. We have thought it wise, too, in a book of this size and type, to cut down footnotes to a minimum; chapter and verse for every statement made are not, therefore, provided. The contents pages are sufficiently detailed, it is hoped, to justify the omission of an index. If, after studying this guide, readers are encouraged to explore for themselves the rather forbidding literature on the subject (particularly the International Labour Office studies and reports) we shall have achieved our object.

CHAPTER I

FACTORY LEGISLATION

1. *General*

FACTORY legislation is a convenient term to describe the government-enforced standards in respect of wages, hours and working conditions which are to be found in most industrial countries to-day. The mere existence of such standards, however, of itself proves very little. There may, for example, be lax enforcement; the area of economic life to which the standards apply may be very limited; and what is theoretically a minimum may, in practice, be treated also as a maximum. A hasty comparison between factory legislation in different countries—such as a foreign visitor might make by reading the abstracts of acts hanging on factory walls—is therefore of little value. With this warning, however, it is worth while discussing some of the general principles which have emerged from world experience in the laying down of such standards.

2. *Maximum Hours and Minimum Wages*

As far as hours and wages are concerned, it is clear that no country, unless it is exceptionally favourably placed, can legislate in these matters without regard to the position in other countries. The limits to its independence of action are set by the following circumstances amongst others. (i) The extent of dependence on foreign trade. Quite obviously, a country which is almost a closed economy has a freer hand than one which depends on an international exchange of food and raw materials and manufactured goods. It is estimated that about twenty per cent (in value) of United Kingdom products go abroad; the corresponding estimate for the United States is ten per cent; the proportion in the case of Germany and the U.S.S.R. is less, and is getting smaller year by year. A country's dependence on foreign trade, can, of course, be modified by government policy—tariffs and quotas can be applied, goods formerly imported can be produced at home. Whatever the main reason for imposing a tariff or quota in any given case, it is often alleged to be a necessary accompaniment to high legal standards in the matter of wages and hours. Unfortunately, however, restrictions on international trade tend to mean a less advantageous use of available resources, so that the minimum wages laid down by law may be subject to an invisible shrinkage, due to the reduced purchasing power of money. In which case legislators who hope to establish or maintain decent wages and conditions of work by erecting tariffs may find they are chasing a shadow. This is not to suggest, of course, that the protection of standards of living afforded by tariffs is always unreal. It may be very real, for example, when it takes the form of preventing a temporary influx of cheap goods; or when it allows a promising infant industry to reach maturity.

The hardships involved in a high degree of dependence on foreign trade are, however, seen in their most acute form where protection of this kind cannot, in the nature of things, be afforded. The case of the Lancashire cotton industry, fighting a losing battle in markets outside our control against a country whose standards in hours and wages were so low as to make competition impossible, is too well known to need further emphasis. It is, however, worth while drawing attention to certain aspects of this struggle which are important because they are of wider application.

Firstly, there is no reason to look for any substantial modification, in the near future, of the labour conditions obtaining in the Japanese textile industry. Quite apart from the question of the relative cheapness of living, if the girls in Japanese factories find the hours of work too long, they return home and are replaced by others; no volume of public opinion strong enough to secure the abolition of what the Cotton Mission of 1931 called "indentured infant labour" exists as yet. It used to be argued that a country which exported goods produced by sweated labour lost more than it gained, because of the harm to human resources and national well-being involved. This argument may still hold good if a sufficiently long view is taken; but, if other considerations weigh heavily, the long view may never be taken at all.

Secondly, the technique of the Japanese industry is at least as advanced as that in Europe generally. The importance of a trained labour force still holds good in industry as a whole, but it is becoming possible to produce a widening range of products, particularly staple products, with completely unskilled labour. Engineers are learning to adapt technique to the ability of the worker, with the result that mechanisation to-day, instead of helping good craftsmanship to conquer the world's markets, often enables women and children in less advanced countries to displace skilled adult labour in countries of old industrial standing.

Thirdly, it would clearly be impossible to let labour conditions in the Lancashire cotton industry fall far below those obtaining in other British industries. This raises the familiar problem of the relation between "sheltered" and "unsheltered" industries; and though the "unsheltered" industries are naturally the first to feel the effects of the competition of foreign sweated labour, whenever this results in a lowering of standards in these industries, that lowering must, in course of time, have a depressing effect on standards in "sheltered" industries as well.

(ii) The extent of a country's dependence on foreign trade is not, however, the only circumstance setting a limit to its freedom of action in respect of factory legislation. Another circumstance is the extent to which public opinion favours state control or regulation of economic life. The exact division of territory arrived at, as between government control and voluntary action, in the matter of wages and hours varies considerably from one country to another; but it is natural that the area allotted to voluntary action should be smaller in the totalitarian than in the liberal state.

(a) Four Methods

What choice, then, exists as to the *method* by which some sort of minima and maxima in respect of wages and hours can be enforced by the state? Broadly speaking, four methods are in force, or have recently been operative, in different countries to-day. (i) The most far-reaching plan is that of legislation which applies to almost the whole of industry. Thus in the U.S.S.R. a decree of 1927 provided a time limit before which the seven-hour day was to be established in all industries; and the Labour Code of 1922 laid it down that the worker's remuneration should not be less than the compulsory minimum wage fixed for a given period by the competent state authorities for the class of work in question.[1] France has recently adopted the same plan. The forty-hour week is established in all employments except agriculture, no corresponding diminution in wages being allowed; application to individual trades and regions, however, takes place by Ministerial decree, after consultation with representatives of those involved. The proposed United States plan involves the laying down, in Federal legislation, of maximum hours and minimum wages; and the adjustment of these standards, regionally and by industry, by a Labor Standards Board. Finally, certain States of North and South America have for some time had legal minimum wages of general application; but these minima tended to be low, and of little practical importance.[2]   (It should be mentioned that the fixing of maximum hours does not, as a rule, mean that these hours can in no case be exceeded; but that, if permission is given to exceed them, overtime rates must be paid.)

Failure of other countries to adopt this plan is not hard to explain. Legislative machinery is notoriously slow and cumbersome in action; and it is felt that difficulties would therefore arise in changing the legal standards rapidly enough to suit the changing needs of modern production. It is arguable that this method of fixing legal minima, where effective, tends to hamper

[1] In practice the piece rates laid down in collective agreements, which cover the whole of Russian industry, are now the effective minima, however.

[2] A. F. Lucas, *The Legal Minimum Wage in Massachusetts* (supplement to *Annals of the American Academy of Political Science*, March 1927); and V. F. Morris, *Oregon's Experiments in Minimum Wage Legislation*, may be consulted.

industry in adapting itself to the needs of a world market; and that it is therefore most suited to states which are to a large extent self-supporting. This plan can be modified by delegating wage-fixing powers to a central wages commission; but the position is not thereby fundamentally changed.

(ii) The legislature can delegate its powers of wage and hour regulation to arbitration boards. Such boards existed in many countries during the War; until 1933 in Germany; and still exist in New Zealand, Australia, and certain other countries. It was not as a rule intended, when these boards were set up, that they should fix the general wage level—they were established for the purpose of settling disputes.[1] But when, in order to make them a more effective agency in the settling of disputes, they were vested with powers of giving binding awards, it soon came about that wages in most branches of industry were fixed, directly or indirectly, by these boards. Experience in Germany and Australasia suggests that, in practice, compulsory awards by arbitration boards may introduce almost as much rigidity into the economic structure as the laying down of general minimum wages by legal enactment. The deciding factor is therefore, in this as in many other cases, the degree of flexibility which a country's position —both in respect of dependence on foreign trade and willingness to control economic activities—makes it desirable to maintain.

(iii) It is convenient to call the third method that of "Codes of Fair Competition." The American National

[1] In New Zealand's Industrial Conciliation and Arbitration Amendment Act, 1936 (which re-introduces compulsory arbitration) it is, however, expressly stated that the fixing of basic rates of wages, and the provision of a forty-hour week, for all workers covered by awards and agreements is intended.

Industrial Recovery Act provided for the formulation of these codes for individual industries. They were sets of rules for the conduct of industry and, though the topics covered varied, all codes had to provide minimum rates of wages, maximum working hours, and the right of workers to bargain collectively. The procedure was that the President "approved" codes submitted to him by bodies claiming to represent the parties concerned; failure of the parties to agree, or to put forward a code, meant that one would be prescribed by the President; in either case the codes were legally binding. This novel method of laying down legal standards formed a kind of half-way house between general legislation or arbitration board action on the one hand, and normal collective bargaining on the other. The experiment was of short duration, however; for in May, 1935, the delegation of legislative power involved was declared by the Supreme Court to be unconstitutional. Nor was an adequate loophole left for the retention of the codes without this delegation; for it was made clear that the Supreme Court also regarded them as a form of interference with the internal affairs of the constituent states not covered by the "inter-state commerce" clause. Accordingly only the right to bargain collectively was retained in law; this being incorporated in the National Labor Relations ("Wagner") Act, which the Supreme Court unexpectedly declared to be constitutional in April, 1937. Some of the codes were retained voluntarily, however, thus taking on the character of ordinary collective agreements.

Meanwhile in France provision has been made for compulsory collective agreements which have many features in common with the American "Codes of

Fair Competition"; the initiative, however, lies wholly with organized workers and employers. When requested to do so by any syndical organization of workers or employers the Minister of Labour has to set up a mixed commission, which shall draw up a collective agreement for the branch of industry concerned, either on a regional or national basis; this collective agreement must include, *inter alia*, the right to bargain collectively and the establishment of minimum wages; and the Minister of Labour may, by decree, make this agreement binding on all parties. This, like other recent French experiments in social legislation, will be watched with great interest in other countries.

(iv) A fourth method is that of trade boards. This method is more limited in scope than the others. It does not aim at fixing national minima for the whole of industry; nor is it, except incidentally, a means of settling trade disputes. Its object is the elimination of those conditions of work which we associate with the term "sweated labour". In theory, it is true, trade boards might be set up for all industries, in which case they would resemble more comprehensive methods; but in practice their application has always been limited to certain trades.

Trade boards have been set up in Great Britain, Germany, Austria, France, Norway, Australasia and certain American States. They were first established in Australia and New Zealand at the end of last century. The first European country to follow their example was Great Britain, and it is here that the trade board system has received its widest application. In fact the only limit to their institution in this country is the requirement that the trade concerned should fulfil certain conditions—wages must be abnormally low, and there must exist no adequate machinery for collective bargaining.[1] Before a trade board is set up, however, an inquiry is held, on the basis of which the Minister of Labour, with parliamentary sanction, acts. Coal-mining and agriculture have, by separate legislation, been provided with machinery of the same general type.[2]

These boards—composed of employers, workers and independent members, all of whom are nominated by the Ministry—are empowered to fix minimum wages and maximum hours; to fine employers for contravention of their awards; and, through their officers, to inspect factories for the purpose of ensuring that their awards are being adhered to. Their work is not as difficult as that of boards fixing wages in non-sweated trades, or for industry generally, however. The trades with which they have to deal are not, for the most part, dependent on exports for their existence; and the problem resolves itself into one of providing decent standards, such as workers in the trade would have been able to obtain for themselves had they been properly organized. The boards can therefore confine their attention to the social, as distinct from the economic, problems of wage-fixing. Even if the conditions they lay down do seriously hamper a trade, the opinion is widely held that a trade which cannot provide reasonable wages for its workers will be no great loss to the country. In practice, however, R. H. Tawney was able to show, as long ago as 1914-15, that in those trades in which the system was applied the increase in the wages bill was counterbalanced by a corresponding improvement in organization and technique; and that the only

[1] Trade Board Acts, 1909 and 1918.
[2] Coal Mines (Minimum Wages) Act, 1912; Agricultural Wages (Regulation) Act, 1924.

firms eliminated were those small ones which had previously competed with better-equipped undertakings by a policy of wage-cutting.[1] Experience since that date has substantially confirmed this view; for none of the British industries in which minimum wages and maximum hours have been introduced has suffered a subsequent relapse attributable to the adoption of that policy.

(b) *The Problem of Criteria in Wage-Fixing*

Whichever method, or combination of methods, be chosen, there remains the further problem of the criteria to be used in fixing wages. Three types of minimum have commanded considerable support. (i) The wage the industry can afford to pay. The criterion of what the industry can afford is useful in certain cases. It must be clearly borne in mind, however, that a low wage level may either be a condition of the very existence of an industry, or it may be due to the presence of ill-equipped and inefficient units in the industry. In the latter case (of which the English chain industry used to be an example) this criterion can safely be applied. In the former case (typified by the Japanese cotton industry) wages cannot be materially increased without serious damage to the industry.

(ii) The "fair wage". This is generally interpreted as meaning that one industry should not pay its employees a wage less than that obtaining in other trades for comparable work, i.e., work of similar intensity, involving a similar degree of skill. This principle, because of the element of comparison involved, cannot,

[1] Tawney, *The Establishment of Minimum Rates in the Chain-Making Industry* (1914); *Minimum Rates in the Tailoring Industry* (1915).

however, provide the absolute standard necessary where wages in general have to be fixed by law.

(iii) The third criterion—that of a living wage—is found in practice to be the predominant one where the general wage level has to be fixed. Dispute as to what constitutes a living wage has centred, amongst other things, on the size of the family to be taken as "basic", and on the allowance, if any, to be made for other than purely physical needs. The difficulties involved can probably best be appreciated by studying the legal decisions on the living wage in a country such as Australia, where the matter is still further complicated by the conflict of Federal and State authorities.[1]

Difficulties of this kind do not, of course, arise if the system in operation limits its activities to the sphere of sweated labour. Trade boards can adopt any of the criteria discussed in fixing their minima, comparison with labour in other employments and consideration of the ability of an industry to bear an increased wages bill being particularly appropriate; but with other wages available for purposes of comparison it is not necessary for a trade board to define a living wage. The trade board system is, indeed, particularly well adapted to the needs of the liberal state with a fair degree of dependence on international trade.

It is possible, of course, for a country which is not prepared to provide legal minimum wages for adult males, to treat women and young persons as a special case, and provide legal minimum wages for them. Certain of the constituent states of the U.S.A. have done so: until recently the attitude of the courts appeared, on the whole, to be that such legislation involved constitutionally unwarrantable deprivation of

[1] G. Anderson, *Fixation of Wages in Australia* (1929).

freedom of contract; in March, 1937, however, the Supreme Court upheld the law provided by the State of Washington, agreeing that it was legal to protect women and minors in this way from conditions of labour which had a pernicious effect on their health and morals.

No discussion of minimum wage legislation would be complete without some mention of payment in truck. This practice has had a long history, and Quarter Sessions Records in this country abound in reference to attempts on the part of the justices to stamp it out. Effective legislation was not forthcoming until the nineteenth century, however, and even then the Acts would in most cases have been evaded but for trade union vigilance; without safeguards to prevent payment in truck, it need hardly be said, the value of attempts to provide legal minimum wages is seriously impaired. Truck payments are still found in some countries—certain firms in the United States, for example, pay their workers in "scrip" which is (except at a heavy discount) only accepted at "company stores", where prices are materially higher than elsewhere.

(c) *International Action*

International action, in the matter of hours and wages, has not so far been markedly successful. With regard to hours, one reason for the failure of efforts to limit them internationally has undoubtedly been that the schemes put forward have either been too comprehensive or too rigid. These mistakes are now realized, and efforts are being made on the one hand to draw up conventions[1] applying to special groups of industries,

[1] See Appendix for definition of this term.

and on the other hand to make these conventions as flexible as possible, to maximise the possibility of ratification. Thus the 1937 draft convention for a forty-hour week in textile industries provides for a transition period during which employers can adjust their methods of working, and sufficient skilled labour can be trained; for the forty hours per week taken to be a long-period average, so as to allow of flexibility as between periods of active and slack business; and for special arrangements in backward countries.[1] With regard to wages, a convention was drawn up in 1927 with a view to establishing minimum wage machinery in trades of the type to which the British trade board system already applied. Although the number of conventions, and of ratifications of conventions, has been disappointingly small, however, the action of such countries as France and New Zealand in introducing a forty-hour week may perhaps be regarded as an indirect result of I.L.O. efforts, and is in any case likely to stimulate international action.

(d) *Limitation of hours without simultaneous provision for wages*

Hours and wages tend, for obvious reasons, to be tackled jointly. It sometimes happens, however, that legislation respecting hours alone is introduced where special considerations seem to demand it. A liberal state with no comprehensive wage and hour-fixing legislation may be led to limit hours in dangerous

[1] These elements of flexibility do not, of course, ensure the acceptability of the convention. Thus British employers' representatives claim that the forty-hour week could not be applied in Lancashire without disaster unless (a) organized workers would accept a two-shift system, and (b) other countries were prevented from lowering weekly wages to correspond with the shorter hours.

trades. Thus in England hours of work in mines were limited as early as 1908, at a time when the adult male's freedom in bargaining on wages and hours was still widely felt to be sacrosanct. Again, since the very beginning of factory legislation in this country, women and children have been regarded as a special case, and the progressive limitation of their hours, their complete exclusion from mining, and the gradual raising of the age-limit for entrance to industry have been the earliest and most accepted features of this legislation. It is well known, too, that the limitation of the hours of work of these "unfree agents" meant in practice (once the limits of the working day had been fixed) that in most trades where they worked in conjunction with adult males, the hours of these workers were limited also.

(e) Holidays with pay

It is only since the war that the possibility of including provisions regarding holidays with pay in labour legislation has been seriously considered. There are, in a capitalist economy, certain obvious difficulties in the way of such a plan. For though in the case of state employees, office workers, and others whose changes of employment are relatively infrequent, the technical difficulties to be overcome are small, and it is largely a question of cost; in the case of industrial labour as a whole the position is complicated by the movement of labour from one firm to another. In France, where a great deal of attention has been given to the subject in the twenties and thirties, and a Ministry of Labour inquiry into existing practice was instituted, organized workers were convinced that the difficulties could be overcome, and organized employers were convinced that the technical problems and the cost were alike too great. However, many collective agreements were arranged which made some provision for holidays with pay for ordinary labour, the minimum period of service giving this right varying widely from one agreement to another. Attempts to get legislation passed always met with obstacles until, in June 1936, an Act was passed along with other social legislation of a far-reaching character. This Act imposed a system of holidays with pay on industry and commerce, the professions and co-operative societies. After six months continuous service, one week's holiday was to be provided; after a year, two weeks. Where work was normally non-continuous, however, and in agriculture and domestic service, the Government was left to determine what special provisions should be made.

In liberal states as a whole, the pre-1936 French position is adopted—that no comprehensive legislation enforces holidays with pay, workers in individual industries being left to bargain collectively in the matter, only special categories of worker (e.g. public employees and shop-assistants) having special legislation. It has to be remembered, however, that even where organization amongst workers is not strong, custom, or the desire to attract workers to a particular firm may (as in the United States) be effective in providing holidays with pay in certain employments. In Australia, Federal or State Courts have often prescribed holidays with pay in their awards. In totalitarian states the tendency has been to ensure their provision by legal action. Thus in Italy collective agreements have by law to make some definite provision of the kind for workers continuously employed throughout the year; and in practice it appears that the holiday granted is never less than a week for a worker with a year's continuous service to his credit. In the U.S.S.R. the Labour Code of 1922, or rather the regulations issued since then to implement it, ensure holidays with pay for all workers, subject to certain "continuous service" rules.[1] If these rules are satisfied an annual holiday of twelve days (or more than this in the case of workers engaged on dangerous or unhealthy work) is provided, and can only be carried over to the following year once. In Germany there is no legal enactment covering this subject for workers in general, but the collective regulations which have replaced collective agreements generally provide paid holidays.

3. *General Workshop Legislation*

Legislation regarding general conditions of work in the workshop stands on rather a different footing from the questions so far discussed. The reason for this is that the cost of introducing shorter hours and higher wages (and, it should be added, social insurance of whatever kind) directly increases the supply-price of the articles produced. In terms of accountancy, this kind of expenditure must be debited to the Profit and Loss Account of a special year, and will thus increase either the operating costs, or overhead charges, as the case may be. But the cost of improving the general conditions of the workshop is generally a capital charge, constituting as it does expenditure which, once incurred, is settled once and for all; in this case the supply-price of the product will not be greatly affected, as only the interest on the capital outlay and the allow-

---

[1] These rules have the valuable incidental effect, coupled with other checks on the worker's freedom of movement, of reducing labour turnover.

ances for depreciation are charged to Profit and Loss
Account, and so influence the supply-price of the product. Indeed the cheapening of production resulting
from improvements in workshop conditions often more
than counterbalances the interest and depreciation
charges involved; and in many cases legislation to
improve these conditions only serves to eliminate
firms whose competitive power is based on undesirable
practices, and improves the efficiency, as well as the
labour conditions, of the trade as a whole. Hence
workers and employers tend to-day to agree on most
questions of this kind and no serious problems arise
except where, through ignorance, employers or governments fail to realize the benefits involved.

Recognition of these benefits is, however, a com-
paratively recent matter, so that in a country such as
Britain, where modern industrialism is of long standing,
factory legislation has had to concern itself with working
conditions also. The fencing of machinery and other
precautions against accidents had to be forced on
employers too short-sighted or too selfish voluntarily
to provide such safeguards themselves; and these, like
other parts of early factory legislation, tended to be
evaded until, after painful experience, an adequate
organization of full-time inspectors was provided.
Later, a beginning was made in enforcing standards in
respect of such things as temperature, lighting and
ventilation; but the difficulty of laying down standards
of general application led to increasing resort, in the
early years of the present century, to a policy of schedul-
ing trades as "dangerous", with the consequent enforcement of special health provisions of limited application.

Meanwhile, however, employers were gradually coming to realize the value of good working conditions; so

that it has come about, in this and other countries, that general conditions in modern factories tend, on the whole, to be better than the minima laid down in legislation. Familiar examples include the provision of baths and canteens; while in continental factories in rural areas kindergarten are frequently to be found. High standards in respect of temperature, ventilation, lighting and general cleanliness are aimed at by employers who have taken to heart the teachings of industrial psychologists; or who, since the War in this country, have studied the reports of the Industrial Fatigue Research Board and the National Institute of Industrial Psychology. International, as well as national, action has proved more easy to obtain in this matter than in others; and the International Labour Organization has been able to achieve some of its most valuable results in this field.

It should be mentioned, with regard to most of the types of legal arrangement discussed under this heading of "factory legislation", that difficulties arise in the matter of determining the kinds of establishment which shall be subject to its provisions. Should the determining consideration be the employment of workers for hire; or the use of non-human motive power; or the right of access of the employer to the premises where work is done? It is generally agreed that, in fairness to every one, as many different types of establishment as possible should be brought within the scope of factory legislation; but in practice persons working in their own homes—either as out-workers or domestic workers or as relatives or friends—have usually to be left outside its scope (except, of course, for legislation of more general application, such as Education Acts).[1]

[1] Outworkers are, however, sometimes protected by trade boards.

Unfortunately these are often the very people who, partly by reason of the insuperable difficulties of unionizing them, are most in need of protection.

A word or two must be added, finally, on the division of territory between the present chapter and the chapter following. There is probably no real permanence about the range of topics covered by the factory legislation of most countries at any given time—if this book had been written ten years ago, holidays with pay would have appeared in Chapter two rather than Chapter one; and if it were being written ten years hence family allowances would perhaps be discussed in Chapter one instead of, as at present, in Chapter two. In these circumstances there must, of necessity, be a certain amount of over-lapping and repetition, and the division arrived at may be regarded as somewhat arbitrary. What we have tried to do, however, is to discuss in this chapter those matters which tend to appear in present-day factory legislation; and to devote the following chapter to a discussion of questions which—though in some countries they may be matters of law—are generally left, rightly or wrongly, to be determined by the management individually or in consultation with the workers.

FURTHER READING

(a) *General*

Numerous articles on the subjects discussed in this book will be found in two places in particular. (1) In the fifteen-volume *Encyclopaedia of the Social Sciences* (1930-35), edited by E. R. A. Seligman, where articles are arranged under subject headings and book-lists are provided. (2) In the International Labour Office's monthly *International Labour Review* where articles cannot, in the nature of things, be arranged alphabetically; book-lists giving a brief account of the contents of books listed are provided in every number. These are probably the best sources for discussion of principles and practice. Up-to-date factual information for many countries can be obtained either from the *Ministry of Labour Gazette* (London), or the *Monthly Labor Review* (Washington).

Of general surveys of labour problems in individual countries there are many. For Great Britain, easily the best is J. H. Richardson, *Industrial Relations in Great Britain* (1933).[1] The French position is excellently described by H. Dubreuil, *Employeurs et Salariés en France* (1934), though recourse should be had to periodical literature for the important changes since that date. The corresponding works for the United States are H. B. Butler, *Industrial Relations in the United States* (1927), and S. H. Patterson, *Social Aspects of Industry* (2nd edition, 1935), which can be supplemented by studies of recent developments, such as W. H. Spencer, *The National Labor Relations Act* (1935), J. P. Harris and others, *Social Security* (1936), and P. H. Douglas, *Social Security in the United States* (1936). For the U.S.S.R., English readers will probably find the most useful work to be S. and B. Webb, *Soviet Communism: a New Civilisation?* (1935). For Italy the most suitable book—though its scope is hardly the same as those so far mentioned—would appear to be U. Borsi, *Elementi di legislazione sociale del lavoro* (1936). There are available short surveys of the same kind for many other countries—such as P. Haidant, *Précis de législation indus-*

[1] The Committee on Industry and Trade *Survey of Industrial Relations* (1926) can also be consulted.

trielle et sociale (1935), for Belgium. For Germany—
which has not yet been adequately treated in a survey
of this kind[1]—and for supplementary information on
other countries, articles appearing from time to time
in the *International Labour Review* will be found indispensable.

(*b*) *Chapter I*
Far-Eastern Labour Conditions

Of the large literature on this subject, the following
may be mentioned:
F. Utley, *Lancashire and the Far East* (1931).
Department of Overseas Trade, *Report of the British
    Economic Mission to the Far East, 1930-31* (1931).
I.L.O., *Industrial Labour in Japan* (1933—with biblio-
    graphy).
F. Maurette, *Social Aspects of Industrial Development in
    Japan* (1934).
G. E. Hubbard and D. Baring, *Eastern Industrialisa-
    tion and its Effect on the West* (1935).
The related problem of the position in India is
explained—more briefly than in the reports of the
Royal Commission on Labour—by M. Read, *The
Indian Peasant Uprooted* (1931), and S. G. Panandikar,
Industrial Labour in India (1933).

Minimum Wages

R. H. Tawney's studies (mentioned in the text);
J. H. Richardson, *A Study on the Minimum Wage* (1927);
and E. M. Burns, *Wages and the State* (1926) are
all excellent. There are also available the I.L.O.,
Minimum Wage Fixing Machinery (1927-1928); D.

[1] W. Schuhmann and L. Brucker, *Sozialpolitik in Neuen Staat*
(1934) does not fully meet this need.

3

Sells, *The British Trade Board System* (1923); and G. Anderson, *Fixation of Wages in Australia* (1929). E. C. Shepherd, *Fixing of Wages in Government Employment* (1923) discusses a related problem.

Maximum Hours

The International Labour Organization, in many of the reports of its Conferences, gives valuable information on hours of work, e.g., *Hours of work and Unemployment* (Report to the Preparatory Conference, 1933). H. M. Vernon, *The Shorter Working Week* (1934), is a good discussion of both the theoretical and practical problems involved. Factual information on holidays with pay will be found in the I.L.O., *International Survey of Social Services, 1933* (2 vols., 1936).

Factory Legislation generally

For general principles and American practice, the fourth revised edition of J. R. Commons and J. B. Andrews, *Principles of Labor Legislation* (1936) and J. B. Andrews, *Administrative Labor Legislation* (1936), should be consulted. Four excellent studies, from different angles, of the British position are F. Tillyard, *The Worker and the State* (2nd edition, 1936); B. L. Hutchins and A. Harrison, *A History of Factory Legislation* (1926); H. A. Mess, *Factory Legislation and its Administration* (1926); and G. Williams, *The State and the Standard of Living* (1936). The legal position with regard to the labour of women and children in different countries is described in two I.L.O. publications—*Women's Work under Labour Law* (1932), and *Children and Young Persons under Labour Law* (1935). An exhaustive study of child labour in the U.S.A. is provided in *Child Labor. Report of the Sub-committee on Child Labor of the White House Conference on Child Health and Protection* (1932).

CHAPTER II

SOME PROBLEMS OF MANAGEMENT

1. *General*

ONCE he has complied with the provisions laid down in the factory legislation of the country concerned, there still remain many problems affecting labour which the employer or manager can settle for himself. He may, by choice or by necessity, arrange many of these questions in consultation with works committees or trade unions; but, despite these limitations, he is likely to have some degree of freedom of action in respect of most of them. An attempt will be made in this chapter to give, in outline form, some account of the modern approach to these questions.

2. *The Contract of Employment*[1]

The legal basis upon which the employer obtains the services of a worker, and the worker works for remuneration is, of course, the contract of employment, which need not normally be in writing. The nature of this contract is not now, in most industrial countries, what it was, say, in the early days of the industrial revolution in this country. Thus on the one hand, it has been hedged round by social legislation of all kinds, so that contracts of employment which contravene any of these

[1] See also the section on individual disputes, p. 90.

statutes became null and void. On the other hand, collective agreements, though they do not (except in certain countries, e.g., Italy) alter the *legal* position, make it unlikely that contracts of employment which fail to conform to these agreements will, in fact, be entered into.

The body of law (including, of course, case law) which the courts—ordinary or special—have to apply in matters of this kind naturally varies considerably from one country to another. We can, therefore, only make certain general remarks about the kinds of question usually covered by such contracts. These include what work the worker may be required to do; the question as to whether wages are to be paid in the event of time being lost for different reasons; the basis on which he is paid (in many countries the tendency is now for the law to insist that the worker be given a statement setting out how his wage has been arrived at); what deductions from his wage are permissible; how his wage is protected in the event of winding-up or bankruptcy; and how, and in what circumstances, his contract may be terminated. This last point raises one of the most important questions connected with the contract of employment —how far does it limit the employer's freedom to "hire and fire" labour as he chooses? With regard to the first part of this question, the employer's freedom is most commonly limited in respect of the taking-on of certain types of person— minors (covering, in countries where military conscription or similar arrangements obtain, those in the twenties as well), married women, and aliens. With regard to the second part, there is usually a list of circumstances in which the employer may dismiss a worker—a list which, on the whole, tends to be longer

in the liberal than in the totalitarian state: and provisions regarding compensation or notice. These latter
provisions are, in Great Britain and the United States,
generally left to voluntary collective or individual bargaining; but an increasing number of countries are
making it legally necessary that notice, or compensation
in lieu of notice, should be given. In all that has been
said about the contract of employment it must be
remembered, of course, that the courts tend to lay great
stress on what is the custom in the trade and district
concerned; so that in trades and districts where, for
any reason, conditions have in the past been relatively
favourable from the worker's point of view, the contract
of employment will continue to be interpreted in a
sense favourable to him.[1]

3. *Selection Procedure*

So far as their working life is concerned, the greatest
happiness of the greatest number of workers would
probably be secured by a nation-wide system of vocational selection. Failing that, however, the next best
thing would seem to be that as many undertakings as
possible should so arrange their selection procedure as
to minimise the number of "misfits" employed at any
time. Satisfactory selection methods are in the interests
of the workers; they are also in the interests of the
management, for obvious reasons. What methods, then,
are likely to be most satisfactory? The general principles suggested by American experience (where a lot

---

[1] An excellent introduction to the subject of the contract of employment is provided by E. Herz in three articles (June, July and August
1935) in the *International Labour Review*. A brief summary of dismissal legislation in different countries is provided by G. T. Schwen-
ning in the *American Economic Review*, June 1932.

of experimental work has been undertaken in this field) are that the taking-on of employees should be entrusted to specialists, and not left to foremen; that these specialists should have at their disposal adequate analyses of the types of work done in the establishment, to enable them to judge the fitness of applicants to perform their tasks; that interviews should be standard in character; that tests of natural aptitude, applied to inexperienced workers, should be so arranged as to place all applicants on an equal footing; and that records of the subsequent history of applicants taken-on should be kept, so that the success of the selection methods used can be judged. In this country these principles are rarely applied as a whole, though there is an increasing tendency to improve isolated parts of selection procedure.

4. *Training*

Existing practice with regard to training in this and other countries varies enormously. Thus in occupations where, for historical or other reasons, a recognized system of apprenticeship has not developed, existing practice is likely to vary between letting new entrants pick up what knowledge they can, but making no systematic provision for their training whatever, to the setting-up by employers of "initiation schools" which new entrants attend for a period before starting normal work. In old-established occupations there tends to be some system of apprenticeship or learnership, though it will probably have been considerably modified incidental to the passage of time. Such a system implies an obligation—written or understood—on the part of the employer to provide instruction, and a corresponding obligation on the part of the worker to serve that employer for a minimum period. Trade unions—for a variety of reasons—have played a part in the determination of the terms of such contracts. The idea of special training for foremen, managers, and others (as distinct from highly skilled workers and the technical staff, who have always had to have special training—either in trade schools within the general educational system, as in this country, or in schools forming part of the industrial system, often found on the Continent) is gaining ground; and it is becoming commoner for large undertakings in this country and the U.S.A. to allow members of their non-technical staff time off in which they can attend (sometimes without cost) specified courses at technical colleges and universities.

It is perhaps worth mentioning at this point that our discussion in this chapter so far has related, in the main, to the liberal state. The logical outcome of the principles underlying the totalitarian state would appear to be that both vocational selection and vocational training should be compulsory and organized by public authorities; though existing totalitarian states, it is true, have not yet gone quite as far as this.

One aspect of training which has come to have increasing importance is its use by exponents of "scientific management" —such as Taylor and Gilbreth. The finding of the ideal set of motions for the performance of a particular job, and the subsequent training of the labour force in the use of these motions, was a fundamental feature of their systems. From the beginning, workers—organized or unorganized—were suspicious of these and other elements of scientific management, which was practised in different industrial countries roughly in proportion to the strength of workers' organizations.[1] Their suspicions were, to a large extent, based on the fact that these new methods of work were almost invariably accompanied by new methods of payment; and that these methods of payment either left the worker worse off than before, or stimulated him to efforts which impaired his health.

5. *Methods of Payment*

This brings us, then, to the consideration of methods of payment. For though legal minima in respect of wages may be laid down, there is usually some choice as regards the method by which payment shall be determined. Pure time-rates, the simplest method of all, suffer from the defect that, though a good worker may of course be raised to a higher grade with a higher time-rate of payment, they do not enable day-to-day differentiation between workers of the same grade on the basis of skill and intensity of work to be made. The nature of the work done may, of course, be the determining consideration in choosing between time-rates and piece-rates; or the choice may be limited by the refusal of organized labour to permit one or the other; but, if the matter is not taken out of its hands in either of these ways, the management is likely to prefer the method of piece-rates. The latter, it may be mentioned, vary widely in type—the payment per piece, for example, may be standard, or may vary inversely or directly with the number of pieces already done, or with the time taken; and even where straightforward piece-rates are unsuited to the process, it may be possible to arrange them on a *group* basis, so that the

[1] Soviet Russia has, however, adapted many of the elements of scientific management to suit her own needs.

remuneration of the members of a group depends on the efficiency of the group as a whole. Piece-rates, then, of whatever type, form a means of differentiating, according to the successful effort put out, between workers in the same grade; and in so far as they are successful in increasing the hourly output of a given working force, they involve an important saving in overhead charges per unit of output.

Normally, organized labour stands out against piece-rates and the accompanying tendency on the part of the employer, by "nibbling at the rates", to reduce the worker's remuneration per unit of effort; and the intimate association of these methods of payment with scientific management and the process of speeding-up in industry has rendered the struggle even more bitter. For in answer to the claim that the standardization of motions, the introduction of moving belts and so on lessen the drudgery of labour and eliminate wasted effort, the worker is able to point not only to the increasing nervous strain to which he is subjected, but also to readjustments of piece-rates which often deprive him of the tangible benefits of the new methods. Indeed the opposition of trade unions to piece-rates is so universal and of such long standing that it is at first sight surprising to find that these methods of payment are the rule in Soviet Russia, and that trade unions acquiesce in this. Nor does the commonest theory advanced— that in a socialist state the management has no incentive to indulge in rate-cutting, so that piece-rates are deprived of their sting—seem to constitute a complete explanation. The position becomes clearer, however, when it is realized that the gradual abandonment of trade union opposition to such methods of payment has taken place during a period when the leaders of the

Russian trade union movement have on several occasions been relieved of their posts for failure actively to support the industrial policy of the Communist Party.[1]

Trade unions are also in general opposition to schemes of profit-sharing and co-partnership. With regard to profit-sharing—which may be defined as the payment to employees (in addition to their wages) of a pre-arranged share of the profits of an undertaking in accordance with an agreed scheme—the advantages anticipated by those responsible for its introduction include the more ready acceptance by workers of improved methods; reduction of labour turnover; the exercise of greater care in the handling of plant; and so on. Objection to such schemes by organized workers is based, *inter alia*, on the following considerations: the frequent use of discretionary powers in determining whether a given worker is eligible to participate; the fact that they make his earnings depend partly on the skill with which a firm is managed, without giving him any control over policy; and the feeling that the worker's loyalty to the *firm* is likely to be secured at the expense of his loyalty to his fellow workers in the *industry*. Co-partnership attempts to meet one of these objections by arranging that the participating worker shall share in some way in the control of the under-taking—either as a shareholder with voting rights, or through a co-partnership committee. In so far as this represents a step towards industrial democracy, it is to be welcomed; but schemes vary so widely in their provisions that discussion of co-partnership would lead us into an examination of individual plans. It may be

[1] For details, an article in the *International Labour Review*, February 1934, should be consulted.

pointed out, however, that any scheme—either of profit-sharing or co-partnership—which involves the payment of bonuses to workers in stock instead of in cash has certain obvious *a priori* objections; it is, for example, clearly preferable, from the worker's point of view, that his savings should be in as "liquid" a form as possible.

Normally, in Soviet Russia as well as in capitalist states, workers in employment are paid according to the value of the services they perform[1] (subject, of course, to this not falling below the limit set by law or by collective agreement); and it is only when they cease to be employed that the question of their varying *needs* is taken into consideration. There are, however, exceptions to this statement. On the one hand, women and young persons are in some countries and in some employments paid less than men for doing the same work; one factor—in addition to their lack of organization—in this lower level of payment is undoubtedly the fact that, as their needs are less, their labour can be hired for less. On the other hand, there is the possibility of paying "family allowances" in addition to normal wages. This latter practice developed amongst employers in certain countries during the period of rapidly rising prices after the War; looked at in one way, it was an attempt, supplementary to cost-of-living bonuses and the like, to compensate the family man for his exceptional losses incidental to rising prices. Employers in a given area or a given industry—on the basis of amount of workers, of man-hours worked, or of wages—would pay into a common compensation (or

[1] This is rather a loose way of putting it—the reader should consult the section on the marginal productivity theory of wages in any of the standard texts for a more exact statement of the position in a capitalist economy.

equalization) fund from which family allowances were paid out; in this way it was immaterial to a particular employer what proportion of married men with families he himself was employing. When a general business depression set in in 1929, however, a tendency was observed to discontinue these arrangements as being an unduly heavy burden on industry; so that governments in certain countries—to prevent labour discontent, to arrest an impending decline in population, or to supplement or replace their own family bonus schemes—were led to make the provision of family allowances by employers compulsory.[1] The line of division between governments which applied compulsion and those which did not was not, however, a liberal-totalitarian line. Thus Belgium in 1930 compelled employers both in agriculture and industry to join an equalization fund; France followed suit in 1932 with a more flexible plan—employers' contributions varying according to the particular compensation fund they were paying into; and in 1934 an agreement between Industrial Confederations of Italian workers and employers that they would share the expense of a family allowance scheme obtained legal force (this was supplemented in 1936 by providing, *inter alia*, for a subsidy from the state as well). In Great Britain, on the other hand, there is no compulsion of this kind, and, as in many other countries, family allowances are not common except in state and similar employments. Both lower payment of women and young persons, and the provision of family allowances supplementary to wages, of course, cut across the principle of "equal pay for equal work". This is one reason why such allow-

---

[1] This is sharply to be distinguished, of course, from the practice of enforcing a minimum wage based on a basic family (see above, p. 11).

ances are not provided in Soviet Russia:[1] some of the expenses involved in raising a family are, however, here as elsewhere, covered by social assistance and social insurance; and graduated state bounties are provided for mothers rearing more than six children.

In addition to the factors calling for differentiation so far considered, attempts are sometimes made to tie the wages of all the workers in an industry to some variable outside their individual control. This is best done by means of a sliding scale. The cost-of-living sliding scale, for example, does something to eliminate the confusing factor of fluctuations in the value of money, and makes it possible for workers and employers to bargain collectively on real, instead of money, wages.[2] Then there are sliding scales which relate the worker's wage to the price of the product he is helping to produce. These are of two types. On the one hand, the wage may vary *directly* with the price of the product, as in the British iron and steel industry and the pre-war British coal industry; in this case workers are given an added reason to restrict output, though the intention is, of course, to make adjustment of wages during the different phases of the trade cycle automatic; one factor in the success of such a plan is undoubtedly the extent to which the price of the product happens to be a good index of changes in the cost-of-living. On the other hand, the worker's earnings may be made to vary *inversely* with the price of the product, a plan adopted in gas undertakings in this country, with a

---

[1] The principle, although it applies as between men and women engaged on similar work in the same undertaking, is not, however, a necessary feature of the Soviet economy—wage-rates vary according to the national importance of an industry.

[2] Where such a plan is widely adopted, however, its possible effect on the amplitudes of the trade cycle has to be considered.

view to giving him an interest in increased efficiency of production.

6. *Hours, Shifts and Rest Pauses*

A further group of problems comprises such questions as hours of work, the adoption of a two- or three-shift system, the length of shift to be employed, the introduction of rest pauses and so on. No attempt can be made here to do more than summarize some of the results of experiments (particularly in this country and the United States) in these matters. It is well known that, where hours of work are long, a reduction in the length of the working week is likely to involve increases in workers' efficiency which balance this reduction. Controversy therefore centres round the determination of the optimum length of working week in a given case; and even when some employers have successfully tried out a relatively short week, other employers may, through nervousness or a feeling that conditions in the industry indulging in this experiment are abnormal, fail to follow this lead. The issue is further complicated by the fact that a shorter week may be advocated not only for reasons of efficiency and making the employed worker's life less hard, but also as contributing towards the reduction of unemployment.[1] The introduction of a two- or three-shift system in any undertaking is usually to be explained by the obvious economies involved— the reduction of overhead charges, due to the more continuous use of buildings and plant; and the greater cheapness of dealing with urgent orders when overtime payments do not need to be made—but experience has shown that the worker's efficiency may also be increased

[1] See below, p. 104.

(by the reduction in hours of work involved) to an extent sufficient to make it possible to pay him the same wage for a shorter working period.[1] It is, in general, a condition of this improvement that the worker should have time to accustom himself to a particular shift; and, of course, as the length of his working period is shortened, his rate of increase in hourly production naturally tends to slacken. It can be shown, similarly, that the efficiency of a spell of work of four hours or more is improved by a break half-way through the spell. More frequent rest pauses are also likely to increase aggregate output in cases where work is either heavy or monotonous. The need for pauses can be tested by the construction of "work curves", in which the output of a worker or group of workers per unit of time is recorded on a time chart; a marked dip in the centre of such a curve, for example, clearly shows the desirability of a break at that point. The success of experiments of this kind is not to be measured solely by straightforward improvements in efficiency, however; they tend to have an important bearing on the reduction of the accident rate, and though this may be looked at from the efficiency standpoint also, it is of interest to us here because it forms one way of reducing one of the risks to which the worker is subject.

7. *Environmental Conditions*

As explained in the previous chapter, legal standard

[1] It may be noticed that, since the Decree of 1927 introducing the seven-hour day, the three-shift system has been widely introduced in Soviet Russia; organized labour in capitalist countries is often opposed to such a system (in this country, for example, it opposes the extension of government permission to work women and young persons in shifts—see a departmental committee's report on this subject, Cmd. 4914).

in respect of ventilation, lighting, and health safeguards, generally leave ample scope for individual
employers to improve these matters. In ventilation
the test is cooling power, which is best regulated by
means of temperature in winter and air movement in
summer. Inadequate cooling power, as in the cases
already discussed, leads not only to a low level of
efficiency, but also to an unnecessarily high proportion
of accidents; furthermore, it accentuates variability of
efficiency as between winter and summer. In lighting,
degree of efficiency and accident rate are associated
with the intensity of lighting, its uniformity, and its
colour. It may be noticed in passing that when due
allowance has been made for accidents occurring to
normal workers as a result of undue speeding-up,
failure to shorten the working period or institute rest
pauses, or to improve environmental conditions; and
for accidents resulting from inexperience or age, as
well as impersonal accidents (such as the bursting of a
boiler); there still remain many which are associated
with some form of personal susceptibility to accidents.
If, by adequate selection procedure or vocational
guidance, workers with a high degree of personal susceptibility to accidents could be given work of a suitable kind, it would obviously be to the general benefit.

8. *Labour Turnover*

Finally, labour turnover forms quite a reliable index
of the adequacy of the management's policy in all the
respects outlined above; for workers can—within
limits which, though often not very wide (e.g. in Soviet
Russia and Germany), allow a little scope almost
everywhere—leave an undertaking where conditions

are noticeably worse than those obtaining elsewhere. It is an index which needs to be carefully interpreted, however; the turnover in an individual factory should be compared with the turnover in that industry and district, in order that its full significance as a symptom of failure on the part of the management in the matter of selection, training, methods of payment, methods of work and environmental conditions may be brought out. Indeed the American practice of splitting-up the labour turnover of a firm into the three categories of quits, lay-offs, and discharges, and dividing-up the first and third of these according to the type of reason given for leaving or being discharged; and then comparing the figures with those for the locality and the particular industry involved, does enable those elements of management policy which are most at fault to be located with a reasonable degree of certainty.

FURTHER READING

Special attention should be drawn to the Reports of the British Industrial Fatigue Research Board (now the Industrial Health Research Board); and to *The Human Factor*, organ of the British National Institute of Industrial Psychology, and other publications of the Institute. From the mass of books in English on the topics outlined in the present chapter, the following have been selected:

J. A. Bowie, *Sharing Profits with Employees* (1923).

P. F. Brissenden and E. Frankel, *Labor Turnover in Industry* (1922).

J. Drever, *The Psychology of Industry* (1921.)

E. Farmer, *The Causes of Accidents* (1932).

P. S. Florence, *Economics of Fatigue and Unrest* (1924).

H. D. Harrison, *Industrial Psychology and the Production of Wealth* (1924).

W. O. Lichtner, *Time Study and Job Analysis* (1921).

G. H. Miles, *The Problem of Incentives in Industry* (1932).

B. V. Moore and G. W. Hartmann, *Readings in Industrial Psychology* (1931).

C. S. Myers, *Industrial Psychology in Great Britain* (1926).

J. E. Powell, *Payment by Results* (1924).

E. Rathbone, *The Disinherited Family* (1924).

S. H. Slichter, *The Turnover of Factory Labor* (1919).

H. M. Vernon, *Industrial Fatigue and Efficiency* (1921).

H. H. R. Vibart, *Family Allowances in Practice* (1926).

M. S. Viteles, *Industrial Psychology* (1933).

H. J. Welch and G. H. Miles, *Industrial Psychology in Practice* (1932).

R. Wilson, *Methods of Remuneration* (1931).

In addition, any of the works of F. W. Taylor or F. B. Gilbreth will naturally be found useful. C. B. Thompson, in *Scientific Management* (1922) has collected together a variety of articles on the Taylor system.

Vocational guidance and related problems are discussed in the I.L.O. publication, *Problems of Vocational Guidance* (1935), as well as in articles in the *International Labour Review*. R. W. Ferguson, *Training in Industry* (1935), discusses the practice of a number of British firms; while the adequacy of the facilities provided by local authorities and other agencies is considered in the British Association for Commercial and Industrial Education, *Report of an Inquiry into Vocational Education after General Education up to the Age of Sixteen*, and in A. Abbott, *Education for Industry and Commerce in England* (1933).

The I.L.O. has issued an *Encyclopædia of Industrial Hygiene,* and *Industrial Environment and Health* (1936).

CHAPTER III

SOCIAL ASSISTANCE AND SOCIAL
INSURANCE

1. *General*

THE need for social assistance and social insurance
arises from the practical inability of the individual
worker and his dependants, for whatever reason, to
engage in their normal activities. Accidents, illness,
invalidity, old age and unemployment mean loss of
wages or increased expenditure or both. The resulting
loss can be estimated with a reasonable degree of
accuracy; the probability of such losses occurring is
technically termed a risk.

In many cases the risk may be reduced if the general
conditions of employment are improved: quite
obviously improved sanitation in factories reduces the
danger of vocational diseases; and, as we have seen, the
shortening of hours of work and similar reforms reduce
the risk of accidents. In fact, legislation (including not
merely factory legislation, but the enforcement either
locally or nationally of adequate health and housing
standards) and management policy between them can
materially reduce many of the risks to which the worker
and his dependants are subject; only in rather exceptional cases, however, can they eliminate a risk
entirely. This is where social assistance and social

insurance come in; for both of them provide a measure of group responsibility for the losses and additional expense involved.

This group responsibility may be provided in one of two ways. Firstly, by the method of social assistance, in which the aid given comes either from general public funds or from private charities, no direct levy being made for the purpose on workers or employers in their capacity of workers and employers. Secondly, by the method of social insurance, voluntary or compulsory, the distinguishing feature of which is that workers or employers or both make some direct contribution to the fund from which benefits are provided. Before proceeding to discuss each of these methods in turn, it may be mentioned that there are those who argue that social provision of either kind should be kept at a minimum—that the worker should be expected to make his own provision against the various contingencies that may befall him or his dependants, and that attempts to take the matter out of his hands must of necessity encourage thriftlessness. Even those who hold these views, however, are forced to admit that *some* social provision must be made—neither charitable persons nor the state are likely to stand idly by whilst people die of starvation, or contract diseases which will spread to others; so that it becomes a question of where social provision should stop, and of what form it should take. In practice, it may be pointed out to those who feel that private and public agencies between them leave little to the foresight of the worker himself, the compensation for loss sustained is rarely adequate, and the worker has every incentive to supplement outside aid from his own resources.

2. *Social Assistance*

(a) *By Voluntary Agencies*

In most countries the earliest effective social assistance was provided by persons and institutions which felt it to be a religious duty to help the unfortunate; and this feeling is probably still the mainspring of voluntary action of this kind, though the motives leading men to behave charitably may have become more complex than they were in the Middle Ages. The position to-day is that the *kinds* of voluntary assistance given, and possibly also the aggregate of voluntary assistance of all kinds, are determined in part by the extent of compulsory assistance and of social insurance. Obviously greater scope exists in the United States than in Great Britain, for example. The disadvantages of voluntary assistance are numerous. The absence of legal title to help leads to a feeling of insecurity on the part of the would-be recipient, and the peculiar relation in which donor and recipient are placed may have harmful effects on both. Assistance of different kinds tends to be allocated, not only according to needs of different kinds, but also according to the whims of those providing the money. Nevertheless, it is arguable that some outlet should be left for the expression of charitable feelings, both by means of personal services and financial assistance; but even those who are convinced of this may feel regret that many British hospitals, for example, should have to eke out a hand-to-mouth existence in the supposed interests of maintaining the voluntary principle.

(b) *By Public Authorities*

Gradually in most countries the public authorities

have come to take over the provision of assistance of various types from voluntary agencies, until to-day there are few countries where the public authorities do not recognize their responsibility for providing assistance of some kind. Thus even in pre-1933 U.S.A., many States provided one or more of the following types: elementary education;[1] non-contributory old-age pensions and blind pensions; aid for mothers and children deprived of the support of the head of the household; unemployment relief of some kind; hospitals; and subventions in aid of house building. At the other end of the scale, the U.S.S.R. has, of course, carried the public provision of social assistance very much further. Great Britain occupies an intermediate position. Elementary education is free and compulsory;[1] non-contributory old-age and blind pensions are provided; unemployment assistance is available for a period for those who have exhausted their benefit rights, and public assistance (covering relief in money or kind, or medical treatment) is available for those who are destitute and are not eligible for other forms of assistance; hospitals are provided by local authorities where voluntary institutional provision is particularly inadequate; maternity and pre-school-age child welfare services are available, though they vary in completeness from one district to another; local authorities have to provide school medical services, and *may* provide meals, in public elementary schools; and both the state and local authorities do something to assist the provision of working-class housing. A noticeable feature of the British position is the lack of permanent central co-ordination of all these services; the most

[1] This is not normally included in the category of "social assistance".

that is achieved is central supervision, through the Ministry of Health, of a good many of them.

3. *Social Insurance*

We have noticed already that the distinguishing feature of social insurance—the second method of providing group responsibilitity for certain losses and additional expense sustained by workers and their dependants—is that workers or employers or both make some direct contribution to the fund from which benefits are provided. It must not be supposed, however, that social insurance is necessarily arranged on strict insurance principles. It may differ from individual insurance—to which those in the higher income groups are accustomed—in one or more of three respects. Firstly, instead of careful adjustment of the premium to the risk and a choice of benefits, premiums (or their equivalent) and benefits tend to be highly standardized. Secondly, where premiums are collected from workers, methods of collection tend to be different—weekly collection is a common practice in industrial assurance, and applies (in a rather different form) in most state insurance schemes also. And thirdly, social insurance, because it is serving social ends, may be subsidized—a circumstance which makes it possible either to adapt workers' contributions to their incomes rather than to the risks involved, or to dispense with contributions from the workers themselves altogether.

(a) *Voluntary*

The need for social insurance of certain kinds was felt sufficiently strongly in most industrial countries to ensure that voluntary agencies did something to meet that need. Trade unions from a very early period insured their members against a few of the risks to which they were subject; friendly societies had this as their main object. Employers anxious to attract and retain the best labour sometimes provided insurance schemes. In neither case, however, was a legal title to benefit obtained by the worker. The proportion of a country's workers covered in this way tended to be small, and the schemes were only designed to cover certain selected risks. Insurance companies, too, though they often did something to provide for working-class insurance needs, were not prepared to handle many of the risks to which the worker was subject. It was possible, of course, for the state to subside trade unions, friendly societies, employers and insurance companies in proportion to their social insurance commitments; but this was clearly no real solution to the double problem of increasing the number of workers and risks covered.

(b) *Compulsory*

The only logical solution was to make insurance against certain risks compulsory. Following the lead of Germany, many countries in course of time adopted this plan. The introduction of compulsion was usually accompanied by the shouldering of a proportion of the financial burden by the state. The necessary funds can, of course, be provided by the state, employers, or workers, singly or jointly. Where it is a joint matter, the actual proportion which any group contributes naturally depends to some extent on the ability shown by its representatives during negotiations, and on the pressure it is able to bring to bear on the government of the day. Whether it should be a joint matter or not is an extremely controversial question. In the U.S.S.R. employers are the sole contributors, a charge representing a fixed percentage[1] of the aggregate of wages and salaries being made on the management. Neither in the U.S.S.R. nor in capitalist countries, however, is it easy to determine where the burden of the contributions ultimately falls. And though we cannot discuss the incidence and effects of such taxes here, it may be mentioned that these contributions have a certain bearing on international competition in the case of capitalist states engaging in foreign trade. For workers' and employers' contributions are likely to involve a proportionate increase in the supply-price of the goods produced or the services rendered; so that the efforts of the International Labour Organization to secure the more general adoption of comprehensive schemes of social insurance may, in addition to guaranteeing a minimum of subsistence to the workers involved, also do something to eliminate one type of "unfair" competition in international trade.

It should be added, before we leave the question of finance, that in most countries where insurance against any risk is compulsory, the benefit to be received by the worker affected is both standard and definite.[2] It may depend on his normal wage, or on the size of his family, and it may be supplemented by his union; but he knows in advance how much he can count upon getting. The one exception to this general rule would seem to be Soviet Russia. Here benefits are graded according to

[1] Which may, however, vary from one *industry* to another.
[2] Except that in many health insurance schemes benefit takes the form of medical treatment and supplies as well as money.

the industry and the worker involved; and though some of this grading corresponds to that found in other systems, a good deal of it takes the form of rewards and punishments—workers who, in the opinion of the works committee, have been slack or restless or lacking in public spirit have their rates of benefit drastically cut down, while workers whose conduct has been praiseworthy have theirs increased; precisely the same characteristics are sometimes found in the voluntary schemes of individual firms in capitalist countries.

Where the principle of compulsion, with the corollary of assistance from state funds, was introduced, it naturally followed that the state closely supervised the administration of insurance. Even if the state did not itself undertake the detailed administration of the schemes, it was obviously necessary to ensure that none of the agencies employed should make a profit (in the ordinary commercial sense of the word); and that the worker should be given a legal title to benefit. Few countries, moreover, were in the position of a socialist state such as the U.S.S.R. which, by starting with a clean slate, was able to provide a logical and consistent plan covering all industrial workers and most physical risks.[1] In Great Britain, in order not to bring to an end the voluntary agencies which had hitherto provided social insurance, the plan of working through these voluntary agencies wherever possible was adopted from the outset in 1911. Thus unemployment insurance, in addition to being provided in state employment exchanges was administered, alternatively, through

[1] The plan has, however, been frequently altered, particularly in its administrative aspects. (See an article by A. Abramson in the *International Labour Review*, March 1935). The disadvantages of the piecemeal growth of the British "system" of social provision are well brought out by H. A. Mess in an article in *Politica*, June 1937.

trade unions willing to conform to certain conditions, of which one was the supplementing of standard rates of benefit; while health insurance was very largely administered through approved friendly societies, with appropriate safeguards. It may not be possible in all circumstances to secure this co-operation between the state and voluntary agencies, however. In the United States, for instance, where powerful insurance companies are strongly entrenched in the field of insurance against sickness and old age, it is hard to see how they can be used as agencies for conducting this business on a non-profit-making basis; and they are not likely to give up these branches of their business without a struggle.

Unwillingness on the part of the state to encroach on the territory of voluntary insurance agencies is likely, of course, to mean that certain groups of workers and certain risks remain inadequately provided for. In this country, for example, as the business of life assurance has been left to private companies, heads of working-class households are not compelled to make provision (beyond the small widows' and orphans' pensions provided along with health insurance) for funeral expenses or maintenance of their dependants in case of death.[1] Under the United States constitution the provision or non-provision of compulsory social insurance becomes a matter for the constituent states,

[1] Those who do make such provision, however, are in a sense insuring against more than one risk—a loan on the security of a life assurance policy, or the actual surrender of such a policy, can be arranged in any emergency. It has to be added, unfortunately, that with many types of policy, the worker who is forced to discontinue his payments at an inappropriate moment may find himself in a worse position than if he had merely put his premiums into an ordinary savings bank. The bulk of industrial assurance in this country is concerned with funeral benefits, and suffers from obvious defects in the matter of lapsed policies and high administration costs.

with the result that the worker's position in this respect varies greatly in different parts of the country; though as the Supreme Court has reached a favourable decision on the Social Security Act (which aims at encouraging states to institute old age pensions and unemployment insurance by subsidies from the Federal Exchequer) large numbers of workers whose insurance needs are at present inadequately met by voluntary agencies are likely to be brought within the range of state schemes. Indeed the United States have hitherto provided an object lesson in the disadvantages of voluntary—and particularly profit-making—social insurances: it provides inadequate protection for optimistic workers on the one hand and ill-paid workers on the other; it tends to be unduly expensive, both because of the predominance of "bad risks", and because of the difficulties to be overcome in inducing workers to insure; and it tends to provide inadequate cover for just those risks where cover is most needed, such as unemployment.

One question still remains to be asked—why not extend the provision of social assistance by public authorities in such a way as to render social insurance, compulsory or voluntary, unnecessary? In theory this could be done, but in practice even Soviet Russia has preferred to provide for some risks by means of insurance (in the sense defined earlier). The advantages claimed for insurance by its advocates in capitalist countries include making the worker feel he has contributed towards his benefit—though this does not apply where he makes no contribution; making industries bear the burden of their own unnecessarily heavy workers' risks—though this does not apply where the scheme is financially one unit; and making it possible to avoid all deterrent provisions (including means tests)—though it may be argued that it ought to be possible to eliminate the deterrent element in assistance also, and so do away with many anomalies.

(c) Special Case of Workmen's Compensation

Special mention has to be made of that type of social insurance known as workmen's compensation. The legal story of workmen's compensation is a complicated one—in this country the onus was at one time on the worker to prove his master's negligence— with which it is not necessary for us to concern ourselves here.   The position to-day is that, in most countries, the employer is held responsible for injuries sustained and occupational diseases contracted by a worker in the course of his employment.   Should the employer be compelled to insure against this liability? In this country he is not compelled to do so.   In Germany, on the other hand, employers are legally compelled to join special associations created for the purpose; these associations levy contributions from their members (the employers) sufficient in amount to cover the cost of compensation paid to workers: a similar plan, thought operating through a single institution, is applied in Italy.[1]   In theory a plan of the latter type would seem to provide greater security for the worker than is provided in British practice, since the employer's insolvency does not adversely affect the worker.   In practice, however, most British employers insure against the risk of accidents to their workers; and even in the case of an employer who had failed so to insure

[1] For details of the Italian plan, an article in the *International Labour Review*, January 1936, can be consulted.

going bankrupt, a claim for compensation would, under English law, have priority over the claims of certain other types of creditor.[1] Indeed, if we looked no further than this, it might not be an exaggeration to suggest that the people most vitally concerned in the choice between one of these methods and the other were those whose business was insurance. It is, at all events, no accident that in this country and the United States, which did not follow the German lead, powerful insurance companies of long standing existed; while in Germany, at the time the decision was taken, insurance business was still in its infancy.

There are other important problems, however, in workmen's compensation. Firstly, although the employer's liability in general may be unquestioned, the worker may lose his compensation as a result of doubt as to whether a particular injury or disease arose "out of and in the course of his employment"; here, it must be admitted, the totalitarian state is able, by its view of the fundamental importance of fitness amongst its citizens, to dispense with quibbles as to the exact circumstances in which a disease was contracted and so on. Secondly, there is the problem of ensuring that the compensation paid will be adequate. Here present-day British practice succeeds in avoiding many of the old injustices. For though the spectacle of a worker bargaining in the matter of compensation with an insurance company is not in any circumstances a pleasant one, the fact that no agreement in this matter is final until it has been registered by the Registrar of a County Court (whose duty it is very carefully to examine such agreements) does preclude the pos-

[1] There is also, of course, the possibility of the insurance company proving insolvent.

sibility of hasty acceptance by the worker of, for example, an inadequate lump sum.[1] Thirdly, there is the question of the speed with which all the preliminaries are gone through and the final compensation made available: in this matter, naturally, the Italian plan of a single national institution which shall deal with the question without the necessity, except in exceptional cases, of recourse to the ordinary courts, has obvious advantages.

Further Reading

For factual information relating to a number of countries the I.L.O. *International Survey of Social Services, 1933* (2 vols., 1936) is indispensable; though it does not include voluntary social assistance. Social insurance is separately treated in an I.L.O. introductory volume, *General Problems of Social Insurance*; other volumes in series M—in addition to the *International Survey* mentioned above—all relate to different aspects of this subject. A. D. Cloud, *Pensions in Modern Industry* (1929), and J. Heinrich, *Die Problematik der Sozialversicherung* (1936), are concerned with principles; and B. M. Armstrong, *Insuring the Essentials* (1932) makes some international comparisons.

For social assistance in Great Britain, a useful little handbook (now out-of-date in some respects) is the Charity Organization Society's *The Prevention and Relief of Distress* (1929). On the same subject G. Slater, *Poverty and the State* (1930); W. H. Wickmar, *The Social Services* (1936); and the various volumes (largely historical in character) by the Webbs on *English Local*

---

[1] It is worth noticing that lump sums no longer form legal compensation in Italy, where pensions, or preferably suitable treatment, have to be provided.

Government should be consulted. For social insurance in Great Britain, P. Cohen, *The British System of Social Insurance* (1932), the *Report* of the Royal Commission on Industrial Assurance (Cmd. 4376 of 1933) and A. Wilson and H. Levy, *Industrial Assurance* (1937), are useful. For social assistance in the United States, G. B. Mangold, *Organisation for Social Welfare, with Special Reference to Social Work* (1934), and F. Cahn and V. Bary, *Welfare Activities of Federal, State and Local Governments in California, 1850-1934* (1936), should be consulted. The literature on social insurance in the United States is large and soon becomes out-of-date; H. Baker, however, provides a useful bibliography in *Social Security: Selected List of References on Unemployment, Old Age, and Health Insurance* (1936); while M. Taylor, *The Social Cost of Industrial Insurance* (1933), and W. F. Dodd, *Administration of Workmen's Compensation* (1936), are not likely to be superceded in their respective fields for some time to come. For social insurance and assistance in the U.S.S.R., S. & B. Webb, *Soviet Communism: a New Civilisation?* (1935), and the books there cited, or N. A. Semashko, *Health Protection in the U.S.S.R.* (1934) can be consulted; and for Italy, U. Borsi, *Elementi di legislazione sociale del lavoro* (1936). Books relating particularly to the relief of the unemployed will be found at the end of Chapter VIII.

CHAPTER IV

TRADE UNIONS

1. *General*

A VERY important part in the struggle to obtain better working conditions has naturally been played by organized groups of workers. On the one hand, political parties representative of working-class opinion have fought in legislative assemblies for the enactment of laws favourable to the working class. On the other hand trade unions have pursued the same ends by the method of direct negotiation with employers. There has, of course, often been a tendency for these two lines of action to converge; but the distinction is worth emphasizing nevertheless. In this chapter we are concerned with trade unions, bodies which the Webbs defined as "continuous associations of wage-earners for the purpose of maintaining or improving the conditions of their employment". Provided the term "wage-earner" is interpreted sufficiently broadly, this still remains the most satisfactory definition.

2. *The Powers and Functions of Trade Unions*

In order to be able to judge the importance of the functions performed by trade unions in different countries, it is necessary also to know something of the legal framework within which they have to act; for it goes without saying that, ever since they first began to be formed, these bodies have only been able to operate within limits set by the legislature and the executive. In short, it is necessary to discuss a variety of questions which can be conveniently grouped together under the heading of the powers and functions of trade unions.

(a) Great Britain

Voluntary associations for a great variety of different objects have always been a feature of English life. When these associations pursued unlawful objects, however, they became unlawful conspiracies; and it was the misfortune of the early trade unions in this country to be regarded in this light—first because they had as one of their purposes the raising of wages, despite the existence of statutory machinery for the assessing of maximum wages; and later because their wage-raising objects were in restraint of trade. When, in the seventies of last century, legislation was passed which prevented their being treated as criminal conspiracies, they could still be treated as civil conspiracies; but in 1906 the law was again altered in such a way as to give them reasonable immunity in this respect also. Threats to their existence or to their funds were only two of the difficulties to be overcome, however; there were also the vitally important questions as to what type of action might or might not be taken during a strike, and as to what types of strike were permissible. With regard to the first of these questions, the record of progress has been a long one, particular interest centring round the problem as to when picketing—a necessary accompaniment of strikes —became intimidation. The present position in this

matter is both complicated and obscure; but it can at
least be said that, by comparison with similar provisions
in other countries, British legal practice does not seem
to hamper the normal conduct of strikes unduly.[1]
With regard to the second question, increasing use has
been made of a doctrine first given legal shape in 1875,
whereby the right of the community to receive essential
services was secured by making it a crime for workers in
those services to come out on strike if their action was
likely to imperil this right; this was extended in 1927 to
apply to all employees of local or public authorities
where such action meant, in the words of the Act,
causing injury or danger or grave inconvenience to the
community.[2] In addition, the Act of 1927 also created
a special category of "illegal strikes", from which the
protection of the 1906 Act in the matter of actions for
civil conspiracy was removed; into this category were
placed strikes "with an object other than, or in addition
to, the furtherance of a trade dispute within the trade
in which the strikers are engaged", and those "calcu-
lated to coerce the government either directly or by
inflicting hardship upon the community". This would
seem to lay open to actions for damages unions and
their members engaging in a general strike, or striking
in sympathy with workers in another industry; but
whether legal proceedings would in practice be
instituted may be doubted.

A further question may be noticed at this point.
Political work has been undertaken by unions in cases

[1] Cunnison, *Labour Organisation*, pp. 46-48, gives a good account
of the position.

[2] Unions of public employees, it may be mentioned, are restricted,
by the 1927 Act, in those they may admit to membership; in the
objects they may pursue; and in the affiliations into which they may
enter.

where legislative action seemed likely to bring about desired improvements; and this work has involved, *inter alia*, paying the election expenses of members of parliament. Their right to do this was first challenged in 1908; the present position is that funds used for political purposes must be kept separately, and that members' contributions cannot be diverted into such funds unless the members involved have "contracted into" that obligation.

It is within these limits, then, that trade unions in this country function. But the account so far given of the hindrances to their freedom of action, taken by itself, would give a very distorted picture of their place in English life. They have become a normal and necessary feature of industry, the bulk of which is covered by collective agreements regarding wages, hours and general conditions drawn up as the result of voluntary collective bargaining between organized workers and organized employers; indeed, where lack of unionization prevents such agreements from coming into existence, other means of attaining the same end are provided by the state. Again, as we have seen, they often co-operate with the state in the provision of certain types of social insurance. They form the normal channel through which the opinion of the workers is obtained in case of proposed changes in industrial legislation, quite apart from the influence they exert through members of parliament whose candidature they have actively supported. They do important educational work, and at Ruskin College, Oxford, future leaders of the movement are trained. Opportunity for the discussion of projects for economic and political reform is provided at the annual delegate conference of the Trades Union Congress. Finally, during a period of emergency—such as a war or the carrying through of an extensive re-armament pro-gramme—their active co-operation with the Government has to be secured at the outset.

The Act of 1927, passed at a time when the country had only recently emerged from the General Strike of 1926, is not likely to be the final definition of the legal powers and limitations of trade unions. The Government then in power believed, rightly or wrongly, that trade unionism was at that time in danger of becoming a rival power within the state; and therefore attempted, in this Act, to limit union activity as far as possible to what might be called trade questions. The circumstances in which the Act was passed, and the intention that lay behind it, have naturally precluded any possibility of its provisions being acceptable to the trade union movement as a whole. It will be clear from the subsequent discussion, however, that even within its present legal boundaries, trade unionism in this country has powers and functions far exceeding in importance those accorded to it in most other states, liberal or totalitarian.

(b) U.S.A.

The development of trade unions in the U.S.A. was, prior to 1933, hampered in a variety of ways. In the first place, the legal position was, from their point of view, highly unsatisfactory. Thus it was still possible to impose the "restraint of trade" ban; strikes for many different objects, once having been declared illegal by the courts, could no longer safely be undertaken; no statute laid it down at what point picketing became coercion, and legal decisions on this question tended to interpret most types of picketing as intimidation. In short the courts, both State and Federal, were unfavourably disposed towards trade unions; and neither State nor Federal legislatures passed adequate legislation (on the lines of the British legislation of 1871 and 1906) to prevent the courts from applying to trade unions and their members certain parts of a body of general law which had grown up, in the main, before the need for unions was widely felt.

In the second place, employers showed both persistence and skill in their fight to prevent the spread of unions. Amongst the weapons employed was the formation of "company unions", established and in practice controlled by the employers; when, as often happened, workers were compelled to join these company unions, or when the individual worker had to sign a "yellow dog" contract by which he undertook not to join a non-company union (such contracts being generally upheld by the courts until 1932), normal unionization was made virtually impossible. Victimization of workers not merely for taking part in strikes, but for being members of non-company unions, was extremely common. Thirdly, the American worker did not take kindly to unionism. Numerous reasons have been advanced for this.[1] Individualist tendencies were naturally strengthened by the opportunities of advancement which existed in a country where labour was the scarce factor of production; by the existence until the beginning of this century of cheap land in the West. Wages, except for unskilled labour, were relatively high; and it was possible to argue that unions, along with other European safeguards against the forcing

---

[1] J. H. Richardson's article in the *Economic Journal*, December 1934, should be consulted for further reasons.

down of standards, were unnecessary. Very often, indeed, when unions did gain a footing, the foreign element predominated—unskilled workers coming from countries where unions were common naturally tended to organize themselves.[1]

An attempt was made, in the "New Deal" of 1933, to remove some of the obstacles to the development of trade unionism resulting from the attitude of employers and the courts. The Supreme Court decision of May, 1935, removed the foundation of the New Deal structure; but in the following July the National Labor Relations ("Wagner") Act re-established some of the collective bargaining provisions which the National Industrial Recovery Act had contained. When the "Wagner" Act, in its turn, reached the Supreme Court, it was allowed to stand. Briefly, its terms are as follows. Certain unfair practices on the part of employers in their dealings with their workers are declared in many cases to constitute, in their effects, an impediment to the free flow of inter-state commerce. These unfair practices include interference with the formation or administration of any labour organization; discrimination designed to discourage membership in any labour organization; discrimination against an employee because he has filed charges or given testimony under this Act; and refusal to bargain collectively with representatives freely chosen by a majority of employees. A National Labor Relations Board is charged—in conjunction with the courts—with the interpretation and enforcement of this law. Two points seem to call for comment. The first is that, in common with other

---

[1] Examples are given by B. N. Stewart, *Unemployment Benefits in the U.S.A. The Advance* (organ of the Amalgamated Clothing Workers of America) was published in six languages.

Federal social legislation, this attempt to provide for normal collective bargaining has to rest on a precarious and unsatisfactory foundation—the "inter-state commerce" clause of the United States constitution. The second is that many practical difficulties seem to be involved in applying the Act. Are employers who bargain collectively, but refuse to enter into a written agreement, breaking the law? In view of the ease with which employees may be discharged for a whole variety of reasons, is this Act likely to succeed in preventing dismissals for union activity, filing charges or giving testimony? It is still too early to answer these and other questions. In spite of its obvious defects, however, it seems likely that this Act will promote the growth of unions. It also has an important bearing on their form and basis—company unions, if their constitutions are suitably revised, can still exist; but the Board's right to determine what unit of organization is appropriate in the circumstances is likely to tell in favour of industrial, as distinct from either craft or company, unionism. The position of trade unions in the United States to-day, it is clear, though it represents a big improvement on their pre-1933 position, remains distinctly less favourable than their position in Great Britain.[1]

(c) France

The development of trade unionism in France has been rather different in character from its development in this country or in Germany.[2] To know that the

[1] It should be mentioned that legislation analagous in certain respects to the "Wagner" Act, had been applied to the railway industry prior to 1933.
[2] See below, p. 63.

right of workers to organize themselves and to make use of the strike weapon was finally made explicit in 1884, does not of itself tell us much.   It is more important to realize that, before the War, unions existed mainly to engage in direct struggles with employers; that few of them, accordingly, provided unemployment, sickness or similar benefits (with the natural result that they suffered from widely fluctuating membership).   The local units retained a large measure of autonomy, and only a small proportion of members' subscriptions went to central funds. The most influential group, known as the C.G.T. (Confédération Générale du Travail) believed, not only in direct action, but also in the practicability in the near future of securing syndicalist workers' control of industry as a direct result of a general strike.   Strikes tended to be violent and, as a result of the frequent calling-in of the military, the C.G.T. was strongly anti-militarist in attitude; and asserted its intention, on the outbreak of war, of calling an immediate general strike. In the actual emergency of war, however, the C.G.T. showed as great a willingness to co-operate with the Government as was shown by its British counterpart.   This collaboration, imposed by circumstances, had a permanent effect on the relations between organized workers on the one hand, and the Government and employers on the other.   Thus, after the War, the C.G.T. took an active part in reconditioning the devastated areas; and organized workers secured a greater measure of representation on the numerous councils and commissions that were set up for one purpose or another. This co-operation, however, did not go unchallenged; a certain body of opinion in the labour movement regarded it as treason, and in 1921 a serious split in the movement was marked by the breakaway of a group of unions to form the C.G.T.U. (Confédération Générale du Travail Unitaire), which was a good deal more "left" in its aims and policy.

A noticeable feature of post-war strikes was the frequency with which appeals were made by the workers to public officials—to the Minister of Labour, prefects, mayors, and so on. Employers, it may be noticed, were on the whole averse to the setting-up of conciliation machinery (such as the British Whitley Councils),[1] and little machinery of this kind came into existence voluntarily; a breakdown of the initial collective bargaining tended, therefore, to mean immediate strike action. The stay-in strike, a recent French development which has spread to other countries, may or may not be of permanent value to the labour movement; its use has been followed in France, however, by the introduction of a complicated system of compulsory conciliation and arbitration—the C.G.T. had for some years been pressing for the institution of compulsory conciliation machinery in all trades, but had not hitherto been favourably disposed towards compulsory arbitration.

It only remains to be added that, as is well known, direct action is favoured by French trade unionism to the theoretical exclusion of indirect action—the C.G.T. remains officially outside politics, and does not give direct financial or other support to parliamentary candidates. In practice it should be remembered, however, that the C.G.T. has played a large part in shaping the social legislation of post-war France, all of which has virtually been drawn-up in consultation with it; and that it is usual for parliamentary candidates

[1] See below, Chapter VI.

who want trade union votes to declare their adhesion to the programme which the C.G.T. invariably puts forward on these occasions.

(d) Germany

The Weimar Constitution of 1918 greatly stimulated the development of trade unions in Germany. For though some of its articles were mere statements of what had already been achieved before the War; and though others were never put into practice (all the articles being of the nature of principles, not enforceable without special legislation laying down the limits and methods of their application), conditions generally were peculiarly suited to their growth. The A.D.G. (Allgemeiner Deutscher Gewerkschaftsbund) appeared to be an extremely powerful organization, numbering in the peak years of the early twenties about 8 million members, and from 1924 onwards about $4\frac{1}{2}$ million; it was, however, summarily and with apparent ease dissolved in May, 1933. Trade unions, indeed, instead of being modified to suit National Socialist requirements as had at first been planned, were abolished, and many leading trade unionists were arrested. A new type of organization, known as the Labour Front, was set up, differing fundamentally from the old.

The interests of employers and workers being, according to National Socialist theory, identical, their separate organization is not permissible. Both are, therefore, members of the Labour Front (except if they are in agriculture or the civil service), membership of which is, in theory, compulsory. The Labour Front is, of course, split up by industry and by area: it is not, however, organized on a democratic basis—if members vote, it is merely for the approval or rejection of a leader-designate; officials of all kinds are normally appointed by their superiors, the leader of the Labour Front himself being appointed by the leader of the Reich. The interests of employers and workers being by hypothesis identical, the Labour Front does not include amongst its functions collective bargaining on wages, hours, and working conditions: it functions, instead, as a distributing agency for instructions from the centre regarding the conduct of trade and industry. In short, trade unionism, in the sense in which we are here concerned with it, does not exist in Germany to-day.

(e) *Italy*

In Italy the transformation of trade unions to suit the needs of a totalitarian state took a somewhat less drastic form than it did in Germany. There are separate trade associations for workers and employers, with Federations (corresponding to the national trade unions and employers' associations in this country) for each of them in each trade. These Federations, however, are united in large Confederations, of which there are four for workers and four for employers, covering industry (including transport), agriculture, insurance and banking, and commerce. These Confederations have wide powers of control over the policy of their constituent Federations and smaller units. The use of the strike or lockout weapon is prohibited by law.[1] In case of a deadlock in negotiations, the appropriate Corporation[2] attempts conciliation; if this is unsuccess-

[1] Except in such a case as, for example, the flagrant disregard of an existing collective agreement by an employer.
[2] For an explanation of this term, see p. 84.

ful, the case must go before a labour court, the award of which is binding on all parties. Membership of these official workers' and employers' associations is not compulsory—other types of voluntary association may exist, provided their objects are not opposed to the principles of Fascism. In practice, however, voluntary associations of workers corresponding to trade unions in liberal states could not pursue their normal objects. The agreements arrived at by the official Confederations and Federations are, of course, binding on all workers and employers, whether they are members of these organizations or not.

(f) U.S.S.R.[1]

A serious cleavage of opinion exists amongst foreign observers of Russian trade unionism. On the one hand, supporters claim that trade unions play a very much more important part in this socialist state than their counterparts in capitalist countries. On the other hand, critics are many of them convinced that Soviet trade unions have become a subordinate part of the state machine, with little real power. Certain questions of fact are not disputed by either side. It is agreed that membership of the unions is open to all grades of workers and managers, and is optional; that in practice about seventy-five per cent of Soviet workers are members; that actual strikes are rare; that all-Union collective agreements of a comprehensive character cover virtually the whole of Soviet industry. In spite of this common ground, however, differences of interpretation and opinion can easily arise. Thus, for example, the absence of strike action despite there

[1] See also Chapter V.

being no law against taking such action may be interpreted as meaning that the legitimate claims of all workers are being met; or it may be associated with the practical elasticity of such terms as counter-revolutionary activity and sabotage. Again, it is possible to comment favourably on collective agreements in which both sides are interested in maximising the workers' rewards; in which one class of workers is not able selfishly to exploit its position at the expense of another class; in which the whole of the product of industry is available for immediate or deferred distribution. It is equally possible, however, to point out that the trade union leaders are, in effect, engaged in bargaining with a monopolist; that the limit set to possible wage increases by the prior allocation of an aggregate wage figure for an industry is a serious curtailment of bargaining power; that they will increasingly be led to accept improved rates contingent on increases in productivity, a potentially dangerous policy which their capitalist counterparts would never sanction; that inability, in practice, to withdraw one's labour, singly or collectively, is a serious bargaining handicap; and that when a policy of speeding-up becomes associated with the attainment of a national goal, it becomes doubly dangerous because of its effects on individuals, and because of its deadening effect on the vigilance of union officials. In short, those approaching this problem for the first time might with advantage combine, in their reading, the works of whole-hearted admirers[1] with those of critical, but favourably disposed observers.[2]

[1] Such as S. and B. Webb, *Soviet Communism: a New Civilisation?* (1935).
[2] Such as Barbara Wootton, *Plan or No Plan* (1934).

3. *Some Problems of Organization and Policy*

Once trade unions have secured legal recognition, and their powers and obligations have been adequately defined, there still remain, in the liberal state, many problems connected with the most effective use of those powers—questions, some of which have already been touched on, of organization and policy. With regard to policy, it is necessary to decide what particular combination of direct and indirect action is best in the circumstances; and what part social insurance and other subsidiary trade union activities should play. And, having arrived at these decisions, the leaders of the movement have to decide what particular form of organization is best suited to the pursuit of the policy chosen. This question of organization includes three problems—the basis of organization, the degree of local autonomy, and the possibility of common action between unions. To take the first of these, it is clear that though the basis of trade union organization is accepted as being the common employment of a group of workers, the term "common employment" covers a number of possibilities. It covers, for instance, employment in a given undertaking, which would suggest a company basis; employment in a given process, leading to the craft union; employment in a given industry, leading to the industrial union; and employment for wages, leading to the general mixed union. In this country the industrial basis of organization now tends to be regarded as the most suitable for effective bargaining,[1] and unions organized on a craft basis are

---

[1] It has the valuable incidental effect of lessening the probability of "demarcation disputes", which are particularly numerous in industries such as shipbuilding, where workers are not organized on an industrial basis.

being, in some cases, gradually transformed. While even in the United States—until recently the stronghold of the company union and the craft union—the industrial union is rapidly, though not without a bitter struggle, gaining ground.[1]   A second organization problem—the degree of local autonomy to be accorded to the smaller units—also has an important bearing on effective bargaining power. For if the local branches are allowed to fritter away their funds in unsuccessful or unnecessary strike action, the union as a whole may find its reserves so depleted as to preclude the possibility of a long strike on a major issue. On the other hand, if the powers of the central executive are too extensive, the wishes of the majority of union members may be ignored altogether. In an endeavour to steer between these two extremes, unions in different countries, and different unions in the same country, have in varying degrees limited the bargaining powers of branches and district committees on the one hand, and limited the powers of central executives (by providing for the necessity of ballots before certain decisions are taken) on the other hand. It is perhaps worth adding at this point that as, in the liberal state, these arrangements normally have no legal sanctions behind them, there is always the possibility that the rank-and-file of a union will in any district take matters into its own hands and indulge in unofficial strike action not authorized by the central executive. This is particularly likely to happen where it is widely believed, rightly or wrongly, that the leaders of the trade union movement have entered into some tacit understanding—detrimental to the workers as a whole—with the Government of the

[1] An article by P. Taft, in the *American Economic Review*, March 1937, should be consulted.

day. This possibility of unofficial action means, of course, that however good the voluntary collective-bargaining and conciliation machinery existing in any industry, and however good the relations between organized workers and organized employers in that industry have been in the past, labour unrest resulting in cessation of work may develop at any time as a result of internal friction within the union itself.

With regard to the third problem—the possibility of common action between unions—this depends in part on the position in respect of the other two. For quite obviously, other things being equal, the greater the degree of uniformity between different unions in their basis of organization; and the greater the degree of centralization within these unions; the easier it is likely to be to get union co-operation. Apart from this, however, the development of trade unionism in most countries has been marked by a growing tendency towards amalgamation and federation. In most countries, too, there exists some central body which, within varying limits, co-ordinates the activities of trade-unionism as a whole. In Great Britain, for example, there is an annual meeting of delegates of unions, the Trades Union Congress, which has an executive arm in its General Council; unions which participate surrender none of their sovereignty, but the practical effect of Congress' or Council's known wishes in any matter is considerable, and there is an increasing tendency to regard this machinery as forming the mouthpiece of British trade unionism.

There are many other problems connected with the organization and policy of trade unions in a liberal state. Should they, for instance, use every available means to obtain the "closed shop", in which union

6

membership is a condition of employment; or should they be content with the ostensibly uniform treatment accorded to unionists and non-unionists in the "open shop"—except, of course, where the latter term is used to cover the entire exclusion of union members.[1] Again, to what lengths should they be prepared to go in maintaining the principle of the standard rate (or, more generally, the common rule). Questions of this kind are discussed in all standard texts on trade unionism, some of which are mentioned in the book list at the end of this chapter. There is one further problem which, in view of recent events, it seems worth stating here, and that relates to the nature of a collective agreement.[2] Collective bargaining may take place between a group of workers and one employer, or between a group of workers and a group of employers. The scope of the resulting collective agreement may vary both in respect of the topics covered and in respect of the area of workers covered. Thus, with regard to the first of these points, its scope will vary according to the nature of the trade, the extent of legal provision in respect of hours, wages and working conditions, and the willingness of employers to include given subjects in the agreement. An interesting feature of the American "Codes of Fair Competition", it will be remembered, was that they had, by law, to cover certain essential subjects. With regard to the second of these points, there is a general tendency for employers to insist, wherever possible, on limiting the geographical scope of a collective agreement, and an equally general tendency for organized workers to demand as

[1] An article on this subject in the *Encyclopædia of the Social Sciences* should be consulted.
[2] An I.L.O. study, *Collective Agreements* (1936), should be consulted.

wide a geographical scope as possible. It should be
mentioned that collective agreements resulting from
bargaining between workers and employers on a
national scale need not mean the imposition of standard
conditions in that industry throughout the country.
A collective agreement should, of course, be written—
the American "Wagner" Act does not make it clear
whether the employer's refusal to arrange a written, as
distinct from an oral, agreement with his workers
constitutes a refusal to bargain collectively or not. It
is morally incumbent on the organized employers and
organized workers involved to see that their members
observe the terms of the agreement; where legal
sanctions are provided, it becomes a case of compulsory
collective bargaining, with all the implications thereby
involved. (We confine the term "compulsory collective
bargaining", it will be noticed, to cases where adherence
to the resulting collective agreement is compulsory.
In our view, therefore, there was compulsory collective
bargaining in the U.S.A. under the New Deal, but not
under the "Wagner" Act.)

FURTHER READING

British trade unionism has been the subject of many
books. The classic works are S. and B. Webb, *History
of Trade Unionism* (revised edition, 1926), and *Industrial Democracy* (revised edition, 1926). Three
smaller up-to-date works which will be found very
useful are J. Cunnison, *Labour Organisation* (1930);
J. H. Richardson, *Industrial Relations in Great Britain*
(1933); and F. W. Milne-Bailey, *Trade Unions and the
State* (1934). Others available include F. Tillyard,
Industrial Law (1928); G. D. H. Cole, *Organised Labour*

(1924); and John Hilton and others, *Are Trade Unions Obstructive?* (1935).

For America there are (in addition to H. B. Butler, *Industrial Relations in the United States* (1927)), J. R. Commons and others, *History of Labor in the U.S.A.* (1918. Additional volumes 1935); E. E. Witte, *The Government in Labor Disputes* (1932); L. L. Lorwin and I. A. Flexner, *The American Federation of Labor* (1933); Dale Yoder, *Labor Economics and Labor Problems* (1933); H. A. Marquand, *Industrial Relations in the U.S.A.* (1934); N. J. Ware, *Labor in Modern Industrial Society* (1935); and W. H. Spencer, *The National Labor Relations Act* (1935).

For France D. J. Saposs, *The Labor Movement in Post-war France* (1931); C. W. Pipkin, *Social Politics and Modern Democracies* (1931); H. Dubreuil, *Employeurs et Salariés en France* (1934); and R. Millet, *Jouhaux et la C.G.T.* (1937), can be read; for Belgium, L. Delsinne, *Le mouvement syndical en Belgique* (1936). For the U.S.S.R., J. Freeman, *The Soviet Worker* (1932); and S. and B. Webb, *Soviet Communism: a New Civilisation?* (1935). Factual information on many aspects of the Soviet worker's life will be found in L. Segal, *U.S.S.R. Handbook* (1936). Incidental discussion of Russian trade unionism is contained in B. Wootton, *Plan or No Plan* (1934). For Italy there is a very detailed study —G. Ferri, *Il sindacato fascista nel diritto pubblico* (1935).

An excellent survey of the position in various countries, now unfortunately out-of-date in many respects, is the series of I.L.O. publications under the general title *Freedom of Association*. Theoretical economic problems are discussed by W. H. Hutt, *The Theory of Collective Bargaining* (1930); and in an article by H. A. Millis in the *American Economic Review*, March 1935.

CHAPTER V

WORKS COMMITTEES AND WORKS COUNCILS

1. *General*

WORKS committees and works councils are to be distinguished from trade unions; for while the trade union generally aims at enrolling all workers in an industry or craft, the works committee is composed of *representatives* of the employees in a single workshop or firm.[1] Such a committee is, in fact, a small group of workers appointed or elected to represent the employees of a particular workshop, irrespective of whether they are trade union members or not. Works committees may, of course, combine together, but the essential difference between them and trade unions need not be blurred thereby.

2. *Types of Works Committee*

Broadly speaking, three classes of works committee may be distinguished. There is first of all what we may call the revolutionary type, generally known as the works council. A second class consists of statutory works councils (Betriebsräte), with rights and obligations fixed by law. The third, or Anglo-Saxon, type has no

[1] Unions of the American "company union" type, not being composed of representatives, are not to be regarded as works committees.

73

legal foundation and is not necessarily revolutionary in its aims, but takes whatever form appeals to those concerned. Works committees of more than one of these types may, of course, exist simultaneously in the same country or even, on occasion, in the same firm.

(a) The Revolutionary and Statutory Types

Works councils play an important part in syndicalist theory. For, as is well known, while state socialists are in favour of the centralized organization of production, syndicalists and guild socialists envisage a certain degree of de-centralization, with trade unions, works councils or guilds as the main directive influence in production. The socialist revolutions of Russia and Germany (1918) were both syndicalist in character. A brief sketch of the part played by revolutionary works councils in these two cases may make the position clearer.

(i) The overthrow of the Czarist regime was followed by the rapid spread of organization amongst industrial workers. The works councils that came into being were, from the start, part of the industrial trade union structure; and, in the early stages of the revolution, the responsibility for production naturally rested largely on this structure.

With the temporary re-introduction of a measure of private capitalism in the New Economic Policy of 1921, however, works councils and unions alike came once more to engage in such activities as fighting to keep up the wages and conditions of their members. When the New Economic Policy was abandoned, with the introduction of the first Five-Year Plan in 1928, it became clear that to let them continue these activities would, from the central government's point of view, make it necessary to meet the current demands of workers at the expense of the capital needs of industry. Nor was it, under the Plan, possible to let them have, in law or in fact, the determination of production in their hands. They have therefore come to have the function of expediting the carrying-out of production plans which, though they may have had a hand in shaping them, are not their own; in addition, as explained earlier, to bargaining for collective agreements and administering social insurance. The part played by works councils (which are now, of course, statutory in character, and remain an essential part of the trade union structure) includes the detailed administration of social insurance, management of canteens and clubs, discussion with the factory management—over whom, incidentally, they have no control—and, above all, the encouragement, by every means possible, of workers in their own unit to excel in productive efficiency.

(ii) In Germany, during the 1918 revolution, it became apparent that works councils and trade unions were in serious disagreement. It happened that, though both were anxious for the setting-up of a socialist system, members of works councils tended to favour immediate action, while members of trade unions inclined towards a more gradual policy. Realizing the impossibility, at that time, of actually abolishing works councils, the Social Democratic Party (which was closely associated with the trade union movement) lent its weight to the "bourgeois" parties in the Reichstag in an endeavour at least to curb the power of the councils. Consequently, though the Weimar constitution provided for a system of works councils, leading on to district councils and a central council to collaborate with the Government, little was done to implement these pledges. The district councils were never formed; and though a preliminary central council was set up, it did not operate as the central committee of the works council system. An Act was passed in 1920, providing for the formation of statutory works councils in all undertakings with more than twenty employees; but the provisions of this Act gave these statutory bodies little real power. Their main function was to protect the workers' interests; but almost the only way in which the Act helped them to do so, was by enabling the works council to be a legal person in suing an employer. They were obliged to assist the management; but only in the case of companies, where they were allowed to elect delegates to the board of directors, was any provision made for giving them any control over general policy. Even here, the plan of delegating powers of taking important decisions to sub-committees was soon evolved; so that full meetings of the board, to which alone the workers' delegates had access, soon lost much of their significance. In short, this experiment in the formation of statutory works councils was hardly given a fair chance; and the disunity of the labour movement, of which this was a symptom, made the success of the National Socialist revolution easier than it would other-wise have been.

Works councils still exist in Germany, but they hardly represent the workers in the sense in which representation is understood in liberal states. The procedure is that the employer (called the leader), after consultation with the foreman of the National Socialist Works Cell Organization of the firm, selects a Confidential Council. The workers then vote for or against this Council. In the event of their rejecting their "representatives", the Trustee of Labour (an official of the

Reich appointed by, and subordinate to, the Minister of Labour) either appoints a new Council, or confirms the one originally chosen by the leader. The Confidential Council so selected acts purely in an advisory capacity.[1]

(b) The Anglo-Saxon Type

Particularly since the outbreak of the War, works committees have increased greatly in number in Great Britain and the United States. There has, however, been no general legislation for the institution of such committees; their development has been largely spontaneous, and their character has varied according to the needs of the case. It looked at one time as though such legislation might be passed in England. Mr. Mander introduced two Bills on the subject; and the second of these, in 1930, provided for works councils with functions similar to the German statutory works councils: amongst other things, they were to discuss questions of dismissal of employees, and were to have access to the firm's balance sheet. It was felt by some of those in sympathy with the principles of the Bill, however, that if employers were forced to accept such a plan against their wishes, their subsequent co-operation would be difficult to secure; while the imposition of a uniform system throughout the country was a serious step to take, when experience of works committees had not been carefully considered and sifted. Subsequent events in Germany, as we have seen, showed fears of this kind to be well-founded. Indeed, it is arguable that legislation of general application would have crippled

[1] For a useful summary, the *Ministry of Labour Gazette*, February 1934, may be consulted.

the successful pioneer work on works committees since carried-on both in this country and America.

As an indication of the lines along which some of these experiments have run, the following summary of what one progressive employer[1] regards as the scope and possibilities of works committees is given. The following four committees might develop into two—one for organizing activities outside working hours, and the other for all other business:

(i) Social Union

Sphere: social activities, mainly outside working hours.

Constitution: includes all grades of management and workers; governing body elected by members irrespective of trade, grade or sex.

Examples of Activities: institution of clubs for sports (cricket, football, swimming, etc.); recreative societies (orchestral, choral, or debating); provision of games, library and so on for use in meal hours; administration of club rooms.

(ii) Shop Stewards' Committee

Sphere: controversial questions where interests of employer and worker are apparently opposed.

Constitution: consists of trade unionist workers manual and clerical, elected by works departments or by trades; sits by itself, but has regular meetings with the management.

Examples of Activities: wages and piece-rates (adjustments within, and interpretation of, general district

[1] C. G. Renold, *Workshop Committees* (1921).

agreements); trade demarcations; manning of machines; ventilation of grievances in any of these matters.

(iii) Welfare Committee

Sphere: "community" questions, where interests of employer and worker are not necessarily opposed.

Constitution: composite committee of management and workers, with some direct representation of trade unions.

Examples of Activities: shop rules, working conditions (such as starting and stopping times, meal hours, night shift arrangements, etc.); accident and sickness arrangements; shop comfort and hygiene; benevolent work (such as collections for charities, hard cases of illness or accidents among workers); education schemes (e.g. works schools); trade technique; new works developments; statistics of works activity; business outlook; promotions (explanation and possibly consultation); ventilation of grievances in any of these matters.

(iv) Staff Committee

Sphere: all questions relating to conditions of employment of staff, and where the interests of the staff, as a class, clash with those of other grades. (Not a channel for the transaction of ordinary management business).

Constitution: consists of representatives of all grades of staff below the directors and managers, and above the clerical workers, elected on any convenient basis; no regular meetings; meets by itself or with the higher management, as and when required.

Examples of Activities: training of staff; war bonuses; staff privileges; terms-of-engagement agreements, etc.

It need hardly be mentioned, of course, that the spirit in which such committees are run is more important than their scope and constitution on paper. It does, unfortunately, sometimes happen that the object of an employer in introducing a scheme of works committees is to obtain a loyal and submissive labour force, and to eradicate what he regards as dangerous socialist tendencies by providing as many opportunities as possible for election or nomination to committees. Finally, it has to be added that other organizations loosely called works committees exist in this country, e.g. Miners' Joint District Boards and Agricultural Wages Committees; as well as Railway Shop Committees and works committees of the Whitley Councils. Some of these, however, are more conveniently discussed as part of the machinery of arbitration and conciliation, which is dealt with in the next chapter.

FURTHER READING

There are not many books in English devoted entirely to works committees, which are usually discussed in certain sections of works of larger scope. The only books in English on the German works council system are C. W. Guillebaud, *Works Councils; a German Experiment in Industrial Democracy* (1928) and M. Berthelot, *Works Councils in Germany* (1924). For English ideals, reference should be made to C. G. Renold, *Workshop Committees* (revised 1921) and B. S. Rowntree, *The Human Factor in Business* (1925).

CHAPTER VI

CONCILIATION AND ARBITRATION

1. *General*

COLLECTIVE bargaining, in which groups of workers and groups of employers or single employers meet and arrange conditions of work (which may, when arranged, be incorporated in a collective agreement, the carrying-out of which each group is supposed to be strong enough to impose on those whom it represents) does not of itself ensure industrial peace. In order to do so, it may need to be supplemented by one or more of three types of action, which can be called conciliation, mediation, and arbitration respectively. Conciliation, as we intend to use the term here,[1] means that mixed committees, representative of workers and employers in equal numbers, (with, possibly, some additional members not acting in either of these capacities) endeavour to adjust differences which have already led, or are likely to lead, to strike or lockout action. It may take the form of the establishment, by outside compulsion or voluntary arrangement, of a permanent hierarchy of such mixed committees within an industry, each committee coming into play at a different stage in the dispute. Such a hierarchy of committees, once established, can, of course, if the parties desire it, also have regular

[1] Governments often use the term in a sense roughly equivalent to mediation.

meetings and discuss non-controversial questions. Mediation and arbitration involve the calling-in of third parties to help in adjusting differences. In mediation these third parties merely use their good offices to bring the parties to an agreement, and make no actual award; in arbitration the third parties make an actual award, which may or may not be binding in character.

The discussion of these types of action, however, involves the use of another ambiguous term—"trade dispute". A trade dispute for our purposes is a dispute between employer and employee; the ambiguity is only seen when the cause of the dispute is examined. For it may arise either in connexion with work done in the past or with work to be done in the future; the former may be either an individual or a collective dispute, the latter is likely to be a collective dispute. A trade dispute may arise, that is to say, incidental to a definite breach of contract or in connexion with the interpretation of an existing contract on the one hand; or, on the other hand, over the drawing-up of a future contract. In the first case it would, in theory at least, be possible to refer the matter to a law court; in the second case a body of generally applicable principles is lacking, and is only gradually emerging from the work—to give two outstanding examples—of the British Industrial Court and the Federal Conciliation and Arbitration Court in Australia.

One final ambiguity has to be mentioned, in connexion with the term "compulsory arbitration". This may mean that it is compulsory for the parties to take their disputes before an arbitration board; or that they are compelled to accept the award of such a board; or that both these things are compulsory. For it is a mistake to suppose that the obligation to go to arbitration always involves the obligation to accept the award. In British coal-mining and railway transport, for example, the parties are obliged to bring disputes which have reached a certain stage before an arbitration board, but are not compelled to accept its awards; while in Germany, before 1933, though there was no legal obligation to go to arbitration, awards were sometimes made binding. To avoid confusion, we propose to use the term "compulsory arbitration" only in cases where, as in Italy, both the appeal to the board and the acceptance of the award are compulsory; cases of the other two types will be described in other terms.

It is convenient to divide our discussion into two sections, on collective and individual disputes respectively.

2. *Collective Disputes*
(a) *In Totalitarian States*

Restrictions on individual freedom of action, in trade disputes as in other matters, are naturally found in their most complete form in totalitarian states. There are, however, differences of emphasis and in the means adopted. Thus in the U.S.S.R. collective disputes, where the state is the employer, are subject to compulsory arbitration; where the state is not the employer, however, conciliation or arbitration is only adopted with the consent of both parties,[1] but, once resorted to, the arbitration court's decisions are binding. In Italy, as we have seen, strikes are prohibited,[2] and heavy penalties are provided for those engaging in

[1] This is one reason why strike action is theoretically possible.
[2] Except in such a case as, for example, the flagrant disregard of an existing collective agreement by an employer.

them. Where the normal machinery of collective bargaining breaks down, conciliation is attempted by a Corporation. For, in addition to the vertical formation mentioned in Chapter IV, trade associations are also grouped horizontally in such a way as to form corporations—organs of the state which have as one of their functions conciliation in industrial disputes (they are, as in the case of conciliation machinery in most states, composed of equal numbers of employers and workers). Where this conciliation is unsuccessful, the compulsory arbitration of a labour court settles the issue.[1] In National Socialist Germany, although strikes are not mentioned in the Labour Law of January 1934, their organization would be dangerous and, on account of the suppression of trade unions, difficult. Furthermore, the Trustee of Labour is empowered, in the event of a breakdown of normal negotiations, to make binding awards.

(b) In Liberal States

Amongst the drawbacks of compulsory arbitration in liberal states, two dangers—that the resulting loss of flexibility may seriously impair export trade, and that a lasting settlement may, if one party is dissatisfied with the award, not be secured—stand out: with regard to the second of these, it may be pointed out, incidentally, that the cheerful acceptance of a binding award becomes, in the totalitarian state, not merely a matter of law but also (because of the element of patriotism involved) a matter of policy. Despite these dangers, compulsory arbitration is sometimes found in liberal states. New Zealand and Australia were pioneers in this

[1] See an article by A. Anselmi in the *International Labour Review* January 1935.

respect;[1] behind the shelter of tariff walls it was found possible to institute, by means of binding awards, a system of minimum wages; despite the prohibition of strike action (which accompanied compulsory arbitration in most Australian States), strikes were not in practice eliminated, however. Their example was not followed in other countries until, on the outbreak of war, compulsory arbitration had to be fairly widely applied; in the combatant countries a prolonged strike amongst armament workers, or indeed in almost any branch of economic activity, might have had disastrous results. In some cases (in Roumania, for example) this part of the war system was retained after the conclusion of peace. France, in 1936, introduced compulsory conciliation and arbitration of a rather complicated type;[2] insufficient experience has, as yet, been had of the working of this machinery to estimate its permanence. Germany had a rather peculiar system of arbitration until 1933, which is worth discussing very briefly. An attempt was made to secure that only those disputes the continuance of which was detrimental to the public interest should be settled by compulsion. To this end a system of boards of arbitration was established, parallel to the law courts, a final appeal lying to the Minister of Labour. One court gave the award and the next higher court considered whether or not the public interest was involved; if it found that to be the case, it was empowered to make the award binding. This reservation of compulsion for exceptional cases, it

[1] In New Zealand compulsory arbitration was abandoned in 1932, but was re-introduced in 1936.

[2] The absence of voluntarily-constructed conciliation machinery in most French trades made it necessary to lay down, in this legislation, the form that the hierarchy of compulsory conciliation committees should take; time-limits are provided for each stage of conciliation, and compulsory arbitration is the final stage.

7

was hoped, would mean that only a small proportion of disputes would be treated in this way; so that the flexibility of the wage structure necessary for participation in international trade would not be impaired. The elasticity of the term "public interest", however, brought it about that these hopes were not fulfilled. Organized employers and workers often found it convenient to obtain binding awards; the public clamoured for them whenever a strike caused inconvenience; and the arbitration courts were often able, because of this elasticity, to provide them. This policy, it may be noticed in passing, had important repercussions on the wage level and on the tariff policy of Germany.

As one would expect, the principle of *laissez-faire* in industrial disputes has been allowed fullest sway, amongst industrial nations, in the United States. Prior to 1933, there was no compulsory machinery; the President himself could mediate, a Federal Conciliation Service supplied skilled mediators, the various States provided similar service, and certain industries and firms had arbitration and conciliation boards of their own creation. The "New Deal" of 1933 provided machinery, in the "Codes of Fair Competition", for the settlement of disputes, though decisions were not binding. Since the Supreme Court decision of May 1935, this machinery has not been replaced; and no procedure of conciliation and arbitration has been provided to correspond with the collective bargaining provisions of the "Wagner" Act—the National Labor Relations Board is only concerned, of course, with the interpretation and enforcement of that Act, so that it has no part to play in collective disputes except in so far as those disputes centre round the interpretation of the Act itself. There seems every likelihood, however, that the deficiencies in the existing machinery for the settlement of industrial differences will be made good by legislation in the near future.

The British system, though it may seem at first sight to be haphazard in character, provides many different types of machinery which are, on the whole, well-suited to the cases with which they have to deal. There are, on the one hand, conciliation boards for special trades. Taking industries where the workers are organized, these include, firstly, boards set up voluntarily by the workers' and employers' associations of particular industries; where these are called National Joint Industrial Councils they are on the model suggested by the 1918 Whitley Committee,[1] special features being that all the workers' representatives must be trade unionists, that regular meetings are held, and that non-controversial issues are also discussed. Secondly, there are what may be termed statutory Whitley Councils; these came into existence, after experience had been gained, by being incorporated in Acts of Parliament (the Railways Act 1921, the Coal Mines Act 1930 and the London Passenger Transport Act 1933); disputes must, after a certain stage has been reached, be referred to these boards, but their decisions are not binding; unlike voluntary Whitley Councils, they include consumers' representatives.[2] Thirdly, under an Act of 1912, Joint District Boards were established in mining, mainly for the purpose of laying down minimum wages for piece-rate workers at bad drifts;

[1] The Whitley structure was intended to be a three-storeyed one, with Works Committees, District Councils, and a National Council. Where, as usually happened, only the National Council was instituted, it often came to function mainly as a body with regular meetings which could *inter alia*, attempt to arrive at an amicable settlement of collective disputes.

[2] Except, since 1935, in the case of the railways.

and fourthly, under a temporary Act of 1934, agreements between workers and employers in the cotton textile industry could be made binding if both parties applied to the Minister of Labour, provided that he were satisfied that they represented majority opinion. Only in the third and fourth cases, it should be noticed, were binding awards provided; and this fourth case was an emergency arrangement to facilitate the reorganization of the cotton industry. Where organization amongst the workers is weak, trade boards are, as we have seen, usually set up; this may, by a very loose use of the term, be regarded as "compulsory a.oitration", but actually it is not, of course, arbitration at all.

In addition to these boards for special trades, however, there is also machinery of more general application. Thus, in the first place, the Ministry of Labour has power to offer its services: there are available, in particular, Chief Conciliation Officers in important areas; these officers virtually hold a watching brief in the matter of labour relations, and are experienced in mediation.[1] In the second place a permanent Industrial Court, brought into being by war conditions, has been retained since then. It only functions when appealed to by both parties, and its awards are not binding; in most cases where it has been called-in, however, its awards have in practice been accepted. Thirdly, *ad hoc* Courts of Enquiry, to be described in a moment, can be set up.

The principles behind the British system of conciliation and arbitration are not difficult to discern. Where the parties to the dispute are reasonably well-matched,

[1] The Chief Conciliation Officer should not be confused with the pre-1933 German "Schlichter", as even Weddingen (*Socialpolitik*, Jena, 1933) has done. The Schlichter was an arbiter giving binding awards; the English official has no power to do so.

labour being sufficiently organized to be able to stand up for its rights, as little state interference as possible is decreed. Instead, the setting-up of voluntary machinery is encouraged, by providing model constitutions for Whitley Councils and in other ways; skilled mediators are provided whenever they are needed; and a permanent Industrial Court is available. Where the parties are flagrantly ill-matched, the whole matter is taken out of their hands by the setting-up of trade boards. This still leaves the trade dispute in which the authority of the government is challenged, or in which the public is gravely inconvenienced, unprovided for. As we have seen in Chapter IV, however, certain types of strike have been made illegal or criminal, particularly since 1927; and an appeal to arbitration has been made compulsory in certain cases. There still remain, however, strikes which, for example, gravely inconvenience the public, or do serious damage to our export trade; and even where these contravene statutes, it may not be expedient to put the law in motion. To meet such cases, the following plan exists. The Minister of Labour may, where he sees fit, appoint an *ad hoc* Court of Enquiry to investigate and report on a dispute; this Court may draw up reports, which must be laid before Parliament and may be published and sold to the public; it may also make recommendations which the parties can make use of if they wish to do so. In this way, by providing the legislature and the public with a reasonably impartial statement of the facts of the case, indirect pressure is brought to bear on the unreasonable party, and extravagant demands are likely to be modified. This machinery is, in practice, reserved for use in cases of special importance, and has been found effective.

3. *Individual Disputes*

There is no sharp dividing line between individual and collective disputes. Collective disputes may arise incidental to a breach of contract, or the interpretation of an existing contract, or the drawing-up of a new contract. Individual disputes normally arise incidental to the first two of these. An individual dispute is, however, to be taken to mean a dispute between one worker, or small group of workers, and the management. Broadly speaking, three methods of dealing with such cases are employed.

The first of these is the use of the ordinary law courts without modification. The questions at issue, involving as they do existing contracts, seem suitable for these courts even though a certain technical knowledge of the industry involved may in some cases be desirable. In practice, however, the ordinary process of law is rarely used. For on the one hand, the sums of money involved tend to be small, so that the cost of a normal law suit would exceed them; while on the other hand, a quick settlement is peculiarly necessary in such cases and the ordinary process of law is notoriously slow.

A second method is that of having special sessions of the ordinary courts or special courts; generally speaking, such courts concern themselves with trade disputes regarding existing contracts, whether these disputes are individual or collective, but we are here concerned only with their functions in connexion with the former. In the U.S.S.R. individual disputes are settled by joint committees of workers and the management; failing a unanimous decision, they usually go before a labour court—a special sitting of a court of first instance. In France, although appeals to the ordinary courts are sometimes permissible, special "Conseils de Prud'hommes" deal with individual disputes; these are composed of a secretary trained in law, and lay members—employers and workers in equal numbers. Conseils de Prud'hommes, adapted by Napoleon from earlier French practice, have been widely introduced on the Continent, and the principles on which they are constructed are broadly the same everywhere. In Germany labour courts, composed of professional judges and equal numbers of employers and workers as lay members, were introduced in the post-war period; but appeals, instead of lying to the ordinary courts, were provided for in the labour court structure itself.

The third method—followed in Great Britain and the United States—is that of letting employers and workers themselves supplement the facilities available in the ordinary courts. In trades in which conciliation machinery has come into existence, the local committees tend to deal with individual disputes; cases which prove to involve important questions of principle, however, can be referred to the national council. In addition, of course, trade unions (and, particularly in the U.S.A., Legal-aid Societies) can help their members to sue employers in the ordinary courts. The absence of labour courts in this country is rather surprising. It has, indeed, been suggested that misunderstanding of the real purpose of such courts lies at the root of their non-introduction; for when a Select Committee in 1856 suggested that they should be set up, it was wrongly assumed that this would mean the introduction of compulsory arbitration in *collective* disputes.[1] Two points regarding the present position in this country

[1] Amulree, *Industrial Arbitration in Great Britain* (1929).

are, however, worth mentioning. The first of these is that, in practice, benefits obtained through trade union action tend to become the property of non-members also—employers are hardly likely, by their policy in individual disputes, to drive their non-union employees into joining unions. The second point relates to trades where organization amongst workers is weak; here trade boards, in performing their function of ensuring, by prosecution if necessary, the carrying out of their awards, are, in effect, acting as Conseils de Prud-'hommes.

FURTHER READING

In *Conciliation and Arbitration in Industrial Disputes* (1933) the International Labour Office has provided an authoritative survey of the machinery for conciliation and arbitration as it existed prior to 1932 in most countries, but not in the matter of individual disputes. (A bibliography for each country is included). For British practice, J. H. Richardson, *Industrial Relations in Great Britain* (1933), is again particularly useful; and the following should also be consulted if possible: H. Clay, *The Problem of Industrial Relations* (1929); Lord Amulree, *Industrial Arbitration in Great Britain* (1929); Lord Askwith, *Industrial Problems and Disputes* (1920); and M. T. Rankin, *Arbitration Principles and the Industrial Court* (1931). Whitley Councils are fully treated by B. Seymour, *The Whitley Council System* (1932), a bibliography of books in English being provided.

H. Dubreuil, *Employeurs et salariés en France* (1934), published since the I.L.O. survey, is again a useful guide to the French position.

CHAPTER VII

THE REDUCTION OF UNEMPLOYMENT

1. *General*

IT has been regarded as desirable, ever since Elizabethan times in this country, to draw a broad distinction between those who are able to work but cannot find employment on the one hand, and those whose inability to find employment is associated with physical or mental unfitness on the other. In this chapter, we are concerned only with unemployment of the first of these general types; and only with this type when it does not take the form of unemployment incidental to a trade dispute. It has to be made clear that, in discussing methods of dealing with unemployment, we propose to confine ourselves, in the main, to the practical problems involved; to enter into monetary and trade cycle theory in a book of this size would be patently absurd. Nor can we expect to consider all the far-reaching implications (in regard to a country's economic life) which a given unemployment policy may have. It is, for example, obvious that policies directed towards the increase of employment or the reduction of unemployment may often have important repercussions on standards of living of the working class as a whole. Thus, to take an extreme case, a country which carries the doctrine of economic self-sufficiency to its logical conclusion may be able to insulate itself against cyclical fluctuations in world business activity; but only at the expense of a reduced standard of living.

A preliminary warning may be given with regard to the unemployment figures published by different countries. For, in the first place, in liberal states workers are generally only classed as employed if they are working for the wages customary in the particular trade or industry to which they are attached; while in totalitarian states the term is more elastic, and can, for example, be made to cover those working in labour camps for a nominal wage. And in the second place, methods of estimating the volume of unemployment vary considerably—figures of "persons unemployed" may consist of those registered at employment exchanges, or of those in receipt of relief; or may (as in the United States) be based on sample inquiries and trade union figures.

Faced with the failure through no fault of their own of large numbers of workers to find employment, governments have adopted a variety of methods of dealing with the situation. Broadly speaking, these methods have been of three main types, according to the immediate object aimed at. Thus in the first place, attempts have been made to increase employment; secondly, to reduce unemployment; and thirdly, to relieve the unemployed. It is worth while discussing these three types of approach in turn.

2. *Attempts to Increase Employment*

Employment can be increased in two ways—by the direct creation of new jobs, and indirectly by an appropriate change in the general wage level. The *direct* plan has naturally always had a wide appeal. Voluntary social workers, for example, anxious to help unemployed heads of families, often feel that the making of work forms the obvious solution of the double problem of ensuring willingness to work, on the one hand, and not injuring self-respect, on the other; and that such "made work" need not, if carefully chosen, involve competing with ordinary labour. It is desirable to distinguish between the types of "made work"[1] that can be provided.

There is, first of all, the undertaking of normal public works. A League of Nations inquiry elicited the information *inter alia* that all Member States were in general agreement regarding the desirability of postponing the execution of such works, wherever possible, until a period of depression, and of speeding-up the execution of future public works at such a time.[2] In practice, however, the actual carrying out of such a policy is often hindered by the need, during a period of business depression, for governments to cut down expenditure to a minimum because of the reduced yield of taxes. Due to lack of continuity in policy or lack of foresight, it may be added, governments have not followed the apparently common sense plan of investing funds raised during a period of prosperity and spending them during the succeeding depression.[3]

Secondly, there is work which is instituted mainly for the purpose of providing training and exercise. A policy of this kind is necessary in highly industrialized countries where unemployed workers cannot be absorbed, even temporarily, by agriculture; and where juvenile unemployment is found. Practically all

[1] American usage gives this term a more restricted meaning.
[2] *National Public Works* (1934).
[3] The technical difficulties in connexion with the investment and subsequent liquidation of these funds could be overcome.

countries with a high percentage of unemployment have provided training centres of some kind. These centres vary considerably in character—in Germany agricultural work (including work of military significance) is their mainstay, in Great Britain physical exercise is combined with technical education; the common factor in all this "made work", however, is that its value, in the first instance, has to be judged according to medical and educational, rather than economic, criteria.

Thirdly, there is what we might call relief work proper. This may be work which is regarded as useful in the long run, or which is frankly of no permanent value at all. The distinguishing feature, from our point of view, is that such work would not have been undertaken, even in the near future, but for the desire to create employment. Work of this kind is open to criticism on two main grounds. The first of these relates to its success in detecting malingerers, and in preserving the unemployed worker's self-respect and industrial capacity. Thus it is not difficult to show that work of the type usually provided is unlikely to maintain the industrial capacity of any but the least skilled; that, when the wage paid is below the normal level, slackness and inefficiency are likely to result; and so on. Sometimes, as in National Socialist Germany, attempts have been made to get round these difficulties by adopting the method of giving state grants to private employers for work which they would not otherwise have taken in hand. A second ground of criticism relates to the financial aspects of such work. Thus the cost of relief work tends to be greater than that of other methods of relieving the unemployed. It is well known that the proportion of the funds spent which goes directly to those who would otherwise be unemployed

varies considerably according to the type of work
undertaken and other factors. If the work is chosen
mainly on account of its direct employment-providing
capacity, and the scheme is well administered, it may
be possible, as in Sweden, to pay out as much as seventy-
five per cent of the funds spent to the workers being
relieved in this way; as a rule, however, the proportion
tends to be much less than this—as in the United
States, for example. This is, however, to take no account
of the indirect employment provided by relief work.
Here the argument has to be extended to consider
methods of financing such work. If it is financed by
taxation, or by loans the service on which has to be met
by taxation, it is arguable (in a capitalist economy)
that this is likely to involve a less advantageous distribution of the national resources. If it is financed by
direct inflation the whole problem of monetary policy
is raised. Whichever method of finance is used, the
question is likely to develop into one of balancing the
beneficial effects on the employment position against
the likelihood of ultimately harmful indirect effects on
ordinary business activity. Amongst liberal states
relief work on the largest scale has been undertaken in
the United States, where favourite schemes include the
development of new areas, the planting of forest belts,
and the construction of roads. In the totalitarian state
the method is popular, too, though in cases such as the
excavation, swamp reclamation and road-building
projects of Italy and Germany, it is hard to tell whether
these projects would have been undertaken in any event
or not.

A fourth type of "made work" is work provided for
industrial workers on the land. Experiments in land
settlement are being made, with varying degrees of

success, in many countries;[1] they generally have the double object of creating work for the unemployed on the one hand, and achieving a better balance between industry and agriculture on the other. In this country, although large-scale schemes have often been put forward (by Lloyd George, for example), little has been done in the matter of land settlement. Experience in the settling of ex-service men on the land after the War, at a time of high prices (which gave way, almost immediately production was under way, to a period of low prices), has left a feeling that the cost of such schemes is prohibitive. The provision of allotments—small plots of from two to three hundred square yards, generally grouped together on unoccupied land near a city, or on land reserved for future building—has, however, gone ahead. A series of Allotment Acts has given power to the authorities to provide land for allotments, if necessary by compulsory acquisition. Everybody who has a parliamentary vote or pays rates is eligible for an allotment, and applications from not less than six such persons must be considered by the authorities. In practice would-be allotment holders form societies—there are at present over a thousand such societies with an aggregate membership of over a hundred thousand—which, besides facilitating the provision of allotments, enable seeds, fertilizers and implements to be bought co-operatively. The social significance of the allotment is, of course, very different from that of the small-holding. For while the small-holding constitutes a full-time job for the unemployed man, the allotment cannot support him.[2] Allotment

[1] Germany and the United States have been prominent in this; some of the American experiments are described in the *Monthly Labor Review*, February 1934.
[2] The allotment holder, of course, remains eligible for relief.

schemes do, however, form a sort of half-way house to land settlement proper. In this connexion group-holding experiments, in which a number of unemployed persons co-operate, are of interest; these, and ordinary small-holdings, are being tried as a means of providing work for families from the distressed areas, the choice of families being based in part on their success in cultivating allotments.

A final direct method of creating work is, of course, that of giving special assistance to employers to enable them to take on more workpeople. Thus the provision of tariff and quota arrangements, for example, may have as its object that of enabling new industries to be started, or existing industries to take on more workers. Tariffs and quotas may also be provided, of course, to prevent unemployment arising. It is generally agreed that no gieat lowering of general standards of living need result if this form of protection is confined, as far as possible, to certain cases—the temporary "dumping" of products at uneconomic prices, "exchange dumping" (whereby the exports of countries with depreciated currencies receive, for a time at least, an invisible bounty), and the potential killing of a promising "infant" industry by established foreign units. Beyond this, however, it becomes a question of balancing the increase of employment and other advantages arising against the lowering of living standards and economically less advantageous distribution of national resources likely to result. Naturally, even if the effect on employment alone is being considered, it has to be remembered that protection of one industry may, by increasing another industry's costs, or by reducing the available spending power of workers, create unemployment; so that the important question is the *net* effect on the employment position. Other types of assistance, under this same general heading, include direct subsidies to individual firms or industries; special assistance —in the matter of obtaining fixed or working capital— for industries in depressed areas; special transport rates; and export guarantees. The *a priori* objections to devices of this kind, and the difficulty of ascertaining their net effect on the employment position, are sufficiently obvious not to require comment. The value of another device in varying circumstances—the provision of "cheap money"—is a subject of controversy amongst trade-cycle theorists.

Experiments in the *indirect* creation of work by appropriate changes in the wage level have been much less common. As an illustration of some of the practical difficulties involved, however, the case of two German experiments in 1929-32 may be taken. Two popular lines of reasoning led to the conclusion that high wages would reduce unemployment. On the one hand it was held that high wages meant increased buying capacity amongst workers, and would induce them to increase their purchases; that this increase in its turn would lead industry to produce and sell and therefore earn more; and that these increased earnings would make it possible to pay still higher wages, and in this way a circle of prosperity would have been started. On the other hand, the same conclusion could be reached by a Marxian route—the fact that the workers do not receive the equivalent of what they produce, but are robbed of surplus value, lies at the root of the recurrent economic crises in the capitalist world; hence if wages could be increased to the point at which all surplus value went to the workers, such crises and the unemployment associated with them would no longer occur. Supported

by reasoning of one or other of these types, the policy
of high wages was preached with enthusiasm in
Germany, and the Coalition Government of that time
experimented in the matter. The Ministry of Labour
confidentially instructed arbitrators in trade disputes to
lean towards a higher wage policy in their awards.
The consequent success experienced by strikers in
getting their wage demands met naturally led to increased use of the strike weapon; and this, apart altogether from the higher wages themselves, hampered
industry—a decline in exports (popularly associated
with the experiment) set in, and unemployment, far
from being reduced, continued to rise. The apparent
ill-success of this first experiment led to a change in the
popular conception of the position. The suggestion
that labour was not being employed because it was too
expensive, with its corollary—that wages should be
lowered—began to gain more general acceptance. An
experiment was therefore tried in the direction of an
all-round reduction of wages and prices, with a view to
lowering costs of production and restoring the competitive power of German exports. It was planned to
reduce prices of most goods by ten per cent, wages by a
similar amount, and interest and rents by larger
amounts. The carrying into effect of this plan, however,
proved to be very uneven. Thus prices that had been
fixed by law (such as certain types of rent and interest)
were easily reduced by the appropriate amounts;
reduction of wages, too, was effected. Negotiations
were entered into regarding the prices fixed by cartels
and combines; but, except in the case of proprietary
articles, little success was achieved. The promised
reduction in the prices of necessities of life was not
forthcoming, and labour began to get restive. The

8

Government therefore decided that an effort must be made to reduce the price of bread. By an unfortunate coincidence, however, the leader of one of the smaller parties constituting the coalition of Chancellor Brüning was a baker; and when he was approached on the lowering of the price of bread, he immediately threatened the withdrawal of his party's support. The carrying-out of such a threat would have involved a ministerial crisis; accordingly the price of bread was allowed to stand, and the whole experiment virtually came to an end. Unemployment had again increased, an increase that was probably partly associated with the serious reduction in the buying power of workers and holders of gilt-edged securities; for the policy represented deflation of considerable severity.

3. *Attempts to Reduce Unemployment*

Professor Pigou has defined the quantity of unemployment prevailing at any time as the number of would-be wage-earners, minus the quantity of labour demanded plus the number of unfilled vacancies.[1] If we take the quantity of labour demanded as given, therefore, the reduction of unemployment becomes a matter of reducing the number of would-be wage-earners; or reducing the volume of work done by individual wage-earners; or bringing down to a minimum the number of unfilled vacancies. It is worth while examining these three types of action in turn.

The general procedure, in action of the first type, is that of singling out certain groups of persons who shall, in future, not be eligible for employment; and difficulties naturally arise in deciding on what grounds any

---

[1] A. C. Pigou, *Theory of Unemployment*, p. 10.

particular group should be discriminated against in this way. Broadly speaking, the only acceptable criterion of exclusion in the liberal state, where all citizens[1] are supposed to be accorded equality of treatment, is that of age. This may take two forms—the raising of the age at which it is permissible for employers to employ young people (generally, of course, associated with the raising of the age at which compulsory education ceases); and the provision of pensions, so that at a certain age it becomes either attractive or necessary to leave one's employment. The first form, as was made clear in this country recently, is not as straightforward as it looks. For, unless subsidies are given, it throws part of the burden on to poor families; industries and trades employing juvenile labour press for "exemptions", without which, in their view, it will be impossible to carry on; and educational problems—as to what type of training shall be given in the additional period at school, for example—complicate the issue. Exclusion on other grounds is, however, practised in the totalitarian state. Thus in National Socialist Germany an attempt has been made, by a variety of devices, to exclude women from the labour market: these took the form of the dismissal, on Party instructions, of girls under thirty years of age in industry; of financial assistance to girls leaving industry to get married; of the limitation of the number of girls entering universities; and so on. Partial exclusion on grounds of birth, and supposed political sympathies, is, of course, found in all totalitarian states; a rather peculiar device, found in Soviet Russia at one stage of its development, was the temporary exclusion of any one who had terminated

---

[1] Special permission usually has to be obtained, of course, by foreigners who wish to compete in the labour market.

his employment of his own accord or been dismissed for a breach of the rules of employment.

Action of the second general type—the reduction of the volume of work done by individual wage earners—also takes a variety of forms. There is, first of all, the carrying out, by organized workers, of a policy of "ca' canny". As is well known, this practice has at different times been adopted by groups of workers in certain trades in the belief that the demand for their type of skill was (at least over a short period) fixed, and that such a policy would prevent dismissals. The idea of its general adoption as a means of combating cyclical unemployment has not, however, received much support. Secondly, the management may spread the available work, during a period of slack trade, amongst those normally employed. It may do so from a number of motives, amongst which desire not to see some of its workers deteriorating through unemployment, and the desire to maintain its labour force intact are probably important; and, if due care is taken to adapt your short-time working to the regulations, the state unemployment insurance scheme's funds can (as in this country, for example) in effect be used to subsidize such a policy. A third possibility lies in the reduction of hours—either by shortening the worker's hours per day, per week, or per year. Such a reduction, unaccompanied by a reduction in yearly earnings is, of course, widely advocated with a view to improving the workers' well-being. Where hours are unduly long, a reduction in hours may, as we have seen, be accompanied by an increase in efficiency per hour sufficient to balance it. Even where improved efficiency is not sufficient to balance the reduction, it may be possible to achieve that balance by other means—as for instance, the introduction of a two- or three-shift system with the obvious accompanying economies.[1] In practice progressive employers, particularly in this country and the United States, have shown that the technical problems involved in, say, the introduction of a five-day week, are not insuperable. Governments, which are increasingly leaning towards the reduction, by decree or by persuasion, of working hours are certainly actuated in part by the desire to reduce unemployment in this way.

Fourthly, there is the possibility of maintaining more workpeople in a given productive unit than are necessary for its effective operation. This may, at first sight, seem a highly unlikely proceeding. There are at least two cases, however, in which it may be adopted. The first case is that of a socialist state, where profitability is not as important or as easily measured as it is in a capitalist state; the policy may, in this case, be adopted for a variety of reasons—for example, high labour turnover may make it necessary to keep a reserve of labour at all points—but, for whatever reason it is pursued, it is bound to have a bearing on the unemployment position.[2] The second and more significant case is that of countries such as France, where an interchange of urban and rural labour is possible. This case is of sufficient importance to merit our going into it rather more fully.

France has not experienced unemployment on the scale found in countries such as Great Britain and the United States. Amongst the factors involved there is, firstly, the lack of reliable statistical data regarding

[1] This is, in fact, what has been done in Soviet Russia.
[2] A parallel case is that of the dock industry in many capitalist countries.

unemployment (except in certain Departments) consequent on the lack of general unemployment relief machinery; recorded unemployment is, therefore, less than it would otherwise be. Secondly, it is well known that relief schemes have a tendency to increase the number of people applying for relief; what Sir William Beveridge calls "administrative unemployment" therefore tends to be of small dimensions in France. But a third and much more important factor is the ratio of persons employed in agriculture to those employed in industry and trade (roughly one to one, as compared with one to seven in the case of England and Wales), coupled with the prevalence in many districts of a system of peasant proprietorship. As a result of this third factor, when industrial unemployment develops in France, some of the skilled industrial workers take less skilled industrial jobs; and many unskilled industrial workers are taken on by friends or relatives with small farms, and manage to eke out a living in that way until the employment position in industry improves again. Clearly this interchange between town and country would be impossible unless, on the one hand, agriculture bulked sufficiently largely in the national life to make it possible; and unless, on the other hand, the farms were in the hands of people who were willing temporarily to overstock their land with labour, and city labour at that.[1] In other parts of Europe where you have small-scale peasant farming, the same interchange of labour takes place. It is found, for example, in certain parts of Sweden; and in certain districts of South Germany. In France alone, among European

---

[1] The interchange itself, of course, and the contacts maintained between town and country workers, prevent the contempt of farmers for town labour being as marked as it is in this country.

nations, has an adjustment of this kind been possible on a national scale, however.

There remains the third general type of action in decreasing unemployment—the minimizing of the number of unfilled vacancies. The only way of doing this (except where the recruitment of labour is taken out of private hands altogether, and workers are allocated to particular employments), is by an adequate system of employment exchanges.[1] There is no longer any dispute regarding the desirability of a national system of employment exchanges. For one thing, where they exist these exchanges can be used as part of the unemployment insurance or relief mechanism—both to pay out benefit, to notify workers of vacancies, and to apply the "offer of work" test to suspected malingerers. Again, they form the appropriate mechanism for large-scale redistribution of labour; they can be used, for example, in transferring workpeople from distressed to more prosperous areas.[2]   It is sometimes difficult, however, to secure a satisfactory division of territory between the national system of employment exchanges on the one hand, and other types of employment exchange on the other. This problem does not arise in the U.S.S.R. or Germany; nor is it serious in Great Britain, where, except in the matter of domestic service, the employments covered by the national system are different from those covered by other exchanges. In the U.S.A., however, there are Federal, State, City, Employers', Trade Union and profit-

[1] Defined by Sir William Beveridge as "offices to which workpeople seeking employment, and employers requiring workpeople, may notify their respective needs".

[2] A special Industrial Transference Board was at one time set up in this country for this purpose, but its functions were soon taken over by the Employment Exchanges.

making Employment Exchanges. In many parts of the country, therefore, there is overlapping, and unemployed workers find it necessary to register at several exchanges at once; but some cities—such as Detroit—have succeeded in organizing their labour market satisfactorily. In this country the labour market is, thanks to the efficiency of the employment exchange system, very well organized;[1] and it may be assumed that few unfilled vacancies exist for any length of time except where there is a shortage of the requisite skill or where there is difficulty in transferring workers and their families long distances. In the U.S.S.R. an efficient system of employment exchanges exists; the organization of the labour market there, however, is greatly helped by the limits imposed on the worker's right to dispose of his working capacity as he sees fit.

There are many other problems connected with the organization of the labour market—such as vocational selection, the provision of special training in skills of which there is a shortage, the forcing of employers to notify vacancies to the exchanges or to accept labour sent by the exchanges—which we cannot take up here. One further point is, however, worth mentioning. The subsidizing of emigration can be regarded, from our point of view, as an attempt to fill vacancies beyond the national boundaries. The bearing of such a policy on the unemployment position depends on the following factors, amongst others: the existence of vacancies abroad, and the willingness of other countries to accept immigrants; the similarity of the work done by those who propose to emigrate, to the work available abroad; and the nature of the unemployment which it is hoped to reduce. It is not difficult to point out that the

[1] The problem of dock labour, however, remains.

unemployed workpeople chosen (if they are adults), ought to be permanently surplus to the needs of the home industry involved; and that the whole question of a country's optimum population, and the trend of birth and death rates in it, ought to be taken into consideration also. It is too readily assumed by the layman that unemployment is a proof of over-population and that, in consequence, emigration is always a suitable policy where a substantial volume of unemployment exists.

These, then, are some of the methods adopted with a view either to the increase of employment or the reduction of unemployment. In practice, of course, each country tends to follow a number of lines of policy, which it believes to be particularly suited to its special needs; and this is appropriate, for types of unemployment within one country often vary widely. It would be absurd, for example, to suppose that a line of policy suited to the reduction of cyclical unemployment would be equally effective in the reduction of technological unemployment (i.e., unemployment resulting from the changing technique of industry) localized unemployment due to the depression of certain industries, or seasonal unemployment.[1]

FURTHER READING

Those who wish to study the theoretical aspects of unemployment should, of course, read the most recent works of R. G. Hawtrey, J. M. Keynes and others, and examine the comments of rival theorists on each other's work in periodicals—the *Economic Journal, Quarterly Journal of Economics, Economica,* and so on. Professor

[1] For seasonal unemployment, indeed, almost the only appropriate policy is the dovetailing of seasonal employments.

Pigou's *Theory of Unemployment* (1933) is, as its title suggests, exclusively devoted to this problem.

The topics discussed in this and the following chapter are fully covered by a study made under the auspices of the Royal Institute of International Affairs —*Unemployment: an International Problem* (1935). Sir William Beveridge, *Unemployment: a Problem of Industry* (new edition, 1930) is still a classic amongst books on British unemployment; and H. Clay, *The Post-war Unemployment Problem* (1929) will also be found useful. For the special problem of public and relief works, adequate information will probably be found in two I.L.O. publications—*Unemployment and Public Works* (1931), and *Public Works Policy* (1935)—supplemented by a League of Nations publication based on a questionnaire sent out to governments, *National Public Works* (1934); while a useful article on American public works appears in the *International Labour Review*, June 1937. Land settlement is discussed, from the British point of view, in A. W. Menzies-Kitchin, *Land Settlement* (1935). An excellent little book on unemployment and tariff policy was prepared by a committee of economists under the chairmanship of Sir William Beveridge—*Tariffs* (1931). For possible expedients to increase employment in special industries and areas, the various co-operative studies undertaken by the economics departments of British Universities in such areas, and the reports of the Special Commissioners, should be consulted. A useful article on reduction of hours and its bearing on unemployment, by T. N. Carver, will be found in the *American Economic Review*, September 1936. Employment exchanges and the special problem of dock labour are discussed, with special reference to British practice, in J. B. Seymour,

The British Employment Exchange (1928); E. C. P. Lascelles and S. S. Bullock, *Dock Labour and De-casualisation* (1925); W. H. Whyte, *De-casualisation of Dock Labour* (1934); and T. S. Chegwidden and G. Myrddin-Evans, *The Employment Exchange Service of Great Britain* (1934). The I.L.O. provides an international study in *Employment Exchanges* (1933). The possibilities of emigration from this country in reducing unemployment are discussed in the *Report* of the Empire Migration Committee of the Economic Advisory Council (Cmd. 4075 of 1932).

CHAPTER VIII

THE RELIEF OF THE UNEMPLOYED

1. *General*

WHEN governments have done all that they regard it
as possible or expedient to do in attempting to increase
employment and reduce unemployment, there remains
the question of the relief of those who still remain
unemployed, though able and willing to work. This
question also arises, incidentally, in the period inter-
vening between the adoption of a given unemployment
policy and its full effect being felt. Before the War,
however, most governments were content to let the
able-bodied unemployed be provided for by voluntary
agencies and by such machinery as already existed for
the public relief of destitution however arising. After
the War, with the de-mobilization of large numbers of
soldiers who could not at first find jobs, various special
forms of money payments were provided for special
classes of unemployed persons; and some countries,
such as Great Britain, were also led to a wide extension
of compulsory unemployment insurance arrangements.
Broadly speaking, the policies in force to-day (apart
from the provision of relief work, which has already
been discussed) comprise voluntary relief arrangements
(with or without assistance from public funds), local
publicly-financed relief of the destitute, and permanent national relief schemes covering those in-

112

voluntarily unemployed, or some combination of these methods.[1]

2. *Voluntary Relief Arrangements*

In the United States, in an endeavour to avoid the institution of what was regarded as a demoralizing system of public doles, the relief of the unemployed has tended to be tackled by the launching of large public schemes of relief work, and by the disbursement of doles in money and kind by voluntary agencies. Some cities—such as Detroit—have, it is true, established systems of public relief for the unemployed; and some states and trade unions and business firms have instituted schemes of unemployment insurance; yet it remains true that quite a large proportion of the relief in money and kind (as distinct from work) provided in the United States has been provided by "charities", which have been responsible both for the collection and the disbursement of the funds. During the depression years following 1929 these charities evolved what was almost a new technique in the voluntary raising of money for charitable purposes; every device was employed—varying from the organization of "social events" to the plan of getting groups of workers in employment to contribute one day's wages per month—and when the success of individual charities' efforts began to diminish, those in a given area joined forces in the organization of "community drives". Large though the sums raised in this way were, however, they were not nearly large enough to meet the needs of those unemployed, estimated to number between twelve and fourteen millions in 1933. And unfor-

[1] The position in the U.S.S.R. is peculiar.

tunately the administration of the funds was often open to criticism. This was almost inevitable because, as many of the charities had special groups of unemployed, and special forms of benefit, in mind, it became largely a matter of luck whether any given unemployed person would receive the type of aid of which he was in need or not. In some district, for example, an Irish Roman Catholic unemployed workman might get assistance in buying his food from one Roman Catholic charity, help in paying his rent from another, and a money payment intended to cover both from an Irish charity; while an equally necessitous worker who did not happen to be either an Irishman or a Roman Catholic might not be able to find any appropriate charity at all. Such a state of affairs naturally called for co-ordination of charities, and in some cities this was done in one way or another. In New York City, for example, the Welfare Council kept a register of applicants for relief, covering all charities, so that overlapping could be avoided; and also kept a separate card index of charities analysed according to the type of applicant they considered, and the type of benefit they provided, so that the most suitable charities to which to send a given applicant could be readily determined. In Philadelphia all the charities joined forces and placed themselves under the common supervision of a central organization which co-ordinated their activities. A further measure of co-ordination was, of course, achieved throughout the United States when, after 1933, more emergency relief organizations were created and Federal and State subventions to voluntary agencies of all kinds increased greatly in amount.

The fundamental objections to relying on voluntary agencies for the relief of the unemployed are obvious.

Thus, so far as the raising of funds is concerned, the amounts collected are generally inadequate; and the burden of contributing is not (except in a very rough-and-ready fashion) adjusted to ability to pay. While, on the side of disbursement, the amounts received by unemployed workers tend to be inadequate and uncertain, and to involve gross anomalies as between one case and another; and the worker has, of course, no sort of legal title to benefit.

3. *Local Publicly-financed Relief of the Destitute*

Most countries (some constituent states of the U.S.A. being exceptions) have made permanent provision for the relief of the destitute out of public funds. Features generally found in relief machinery of this kind include, firstly, the raising of at least part of the necessary funds by a compulsory local rate; secondly, the local administration of these funds (with, possibly, some central supervision); thirdly, different treatment of widows, orphans, the aged and the sick on the one hand, and the able-bodied poor on the other; and fourthly the provision, not of standard rates of relief, but of amounts which, taking into account all the circumstances, will bring the recipients' incomes up to a given level.

Given these features, it is clear that this machinery is unsuited to the relief of able-bodied persons who are unemployed through no fault of their own. To begin with, the deterrent principle thought necessary in dealing with vagrants (whether it takes the form of relief "in the workhouse only", or of test-work such as stone-breaking) is obviously inapplicable; again, to wait until those involuntarily unemployed have exhausted their savings and are destitute before relieving them, which the use of the poor law theoretically involves, is obviously undesirable. Further, it may be argued that serious anomalies result from the method of determining the amount of relief, and from the marked differences in scales from one district to another; and that the receipt of poor relief still tends to carry with it a certain loss in social standing which the fact of being involuntarily unemployed does not justify. Finally, it is clear that, where unemployment is localized, recovery may be retarded by a policy which leaves most of the burden of relieving the unemployed on local shoulders; while mobility of labour is impeded where relief is conditional on the fulfilment of residence conditions.

Existing poor relief schemes, subjected to the strain of providing for large numbers of able-bodied unemployed, have tended to undergo modifications in practice which meet some, though not all, of the objections outlined above. In this country, for example, the Exchequer has made itself responsible for part of the rate burden of depressed industries; and outdoor relief to the able-bodied without test work has had to be recognized, in many areas, as necessary. In France special provision was made to ease the strain on the local relief machinery. It was provided that if, in any locality, the burden of pauperism tended to be abnormally large, due to widespread unemployment,[1] the local authorities might apply to the Department for help; the Department and the central government would then make themselves jointly responsible for the financing of unemployment relief in that locality. In such a case, naturally, a corresponding surrender of

---

[1] The number of workers covered by state-aided trade union unemployment insurance schemes in France has been only about 180,000 for a number of years past.

local autonomy in deciding how relief should be administered takes place; a standard rate of relief is provided, varying only according to number of dependants and cost-of-living in the given city; and the applicant must register at a public employment exchange and accept work offered to him.

4. *Permanent National Relief Schemes*

We have seen already that the failure of employers to employ him is one of the risks to which the worker is in most countries, subject; and that it is possible, in this as in other cases, to insure against part of the financial loss associated with this risk. Before the War public encouragement of such a plan often took the form of what was known as the Ghent system.[1] This involved the setting-up—often by a municipality—of an insurance fund which was used to supplement both unemployment benefits paid out by trade unions and similar societies, and also individual saving against the possibility of unemployment. The British scheme of 1911, however, went a good deal further than this; and applied to certain industries (employing about two and a half million workers) compulsory state unemployment insurance; this scheme being extended in 1920 to cover almost all workers (excluding those working on their own account) outside agriculture and domestic service. In many countries since the War similar schemes have been introduced; sometimes the sequence of events (e.g. in Austria and Germany) was that relief plans

---

[1] This system is still in force in a number of countries—in Sweden and in certain Swiss cantons, for example. For its working in Switzerland, T. G. Spates and G. S. Rabinovitch, *Unemployment Insurance in Switzerland: the Ghent System Nationalised with Compulsory Features* (1931) can be consulted.

financed by inflationary means were introduced in the immediate post-war years, and that subsequently, incidental to the balancing of budgets, these plans were transformed into schemes of insurance. Some of the constituent states in the U.S.A. have adopted state unemployment insurance; and the Social Security Act —which encourages the extension of this practice by granting Federal financial aid—is leading more to adopt it.[1]

There is naturally a certain general similarity amongst such schemes.[2] Benefit is usually a legal right, subject to the fulfilment of certain conditions—waiting for a period of days, having a certain number of contributions to your credit, not having already received benefit for more than so many weeks in the current year, registering at an employment exchange, and accepting any suitable employment offered to you. The amount of benefit varies, in different schemes, according to such considerations as sex, age, number of dependants, wage when last employed, and regional cost-of-living (in this country only the first three considerations are taken into account). It is clear that some of these provisions are incorporated in schemes because of the need to keep disbursements within the limits budgeted for when the rates of contribution were arranged. In other words, if these were not insurance schemes, certain safeguards would not need to be there. The existence of these provisions, however, raises the question as to whether unemployment is really an

[1] This Act aims at providing more than unemployment insurance. Reference should be made to an article by P. H. Douglas in the *Economic Journal*, March 1936; and to one by E. E. Witte in the *Journal of Political Economy*, February 1937.

[2] Apart from the question of contributions, which was discussed in Chapter III.

insurable risk at all. In the first place, the risk insured against should not—according to insurance principles— be capable of being simulated; but though it is not possible to provide any safeguard as effective as the doctor's certificate in the case of health insurance, there is the "offer of work" test which employment exchanges can apply (except in periods of very acute unemployment) to at least some of the applicants. It should be noticed in this connexion that a further safeguard against involuntary unemployment becoming voluntary was to have been, in early plans, that of making rates of benefit lower than normal wages; it is extremely difficult, however, to provide for this and achieve the desired degree of stability in the worker's income at the same time; while the unskilled labourer with a number of dependants is always likely to find little financial difference between periods of employment and unemployment. Secondly, it should not be possible to say in advance which members of a group will sustain the risk; here again, though it may be possible to make such an estimate in some cases, the fact that insurance is compulsory prevents those unlikely to become unemployed from taking advantage of their position. Thirdly, it should be possible to estimate the aggregate risk for the group; this is one of the greatest difficulties, for though it was possible to do so in the case of pre-war cyclical unemployment, post-war calculations have almost always been falsified. In view of this last difficulty, it may be asked whether insurance has any real advantage at all as compared with permanent national relief provisions. The answer, so far as this country is concerned, is that when compulsory unemployment insurance was first introduced here an attempt was made to give it a variety of advantages over other possible schemes. Thus the worker was expected to feel a moral, as distinct from a legal, title to his benefit, since he had himself contributed towards it; and he was dissuaded from making unnecessary claims on the fund by the prospect of a refund at sixty of the excess of his contributions paid-in over benefit received. Furthermore, the employer was to be encouraged to arrange his policy in such a way as to employ his workers as continuously as possible; for a certain proportion of his contributions were to be refunded to him in respect of any of his workpeople who had had a full year's employment. In the post-war period, however, these encouragements were done away with, and workers and employers retained only a very indirect interest in reducing claims on the fund; for the prospect of any reduction of rates of contribution was exceedingly remote. And the spectacle of the dock industry being, in effect, subsidized by industries whose employment policy was above reproach led to a demand that certain industries should be allowed to contract-out of the general scheme and get the benefit of their efficient management; this was not, for obvious reasons, conceded, except in the case of insurance and banking.[1]

Furthermore, as some provision other than poor relief had to be made for those who had recently exhausted their benefit rights, the post-war period saw the adoption of intermediate arrangements—under such titles as extended and transitional benefit and financed by Exchequer loans—in this country; and the imposing of some test of needs was a feature of these arrangements at different stages which marked them off from the insurance scheme itself. Discontent con-

[1] For similar provisions in the Wisconsin State scheme, see R. S. Hoar, *Wisconsin Unemployment Insurance* (1934).

cerning the form taken by this means test in the thirties has been active and widespread. Except for this test, the distinction between insurance benefit and other types of benefit has become increasingly blurred; and simultaneously a transformation has been taking place in poor relief. Altogether, therefore, and taking into account the impossibility of forecasting future unemployment with any degree of accuracy, it is arguable that the advantages of a scheme of compulsory national unemployment insurance, as compared with a permanent national scheme of unemployment relief, are not as overwhelming as they used to be; provided that the funds of the relief scheme are raised mainly during periods of business activity, and that a legal title to relief is ensured.

By some permanent scheme—insurance or relief—it is possible, therefore, to protect the worker against part of the financial loss associated with the failure of employers to employ him. Whether the consequent partial maintenance of his expenditure during periods of depression, which has undoubtedly introduced a certain measure of stability into the retail provision trade in this country, also prevents unemployment as a whole reaching the dimensions it otherwise would, depends on a variety of considerations. There is the question, first of all, as to whether the money spent by the unemployed during a depression merely represents transferred expenditure; or whether this money would otherwise have lain idle. Again, there is the question of "administrative unemployment"—the known tendency of relief schemes to create, by their very existence, a certain amount of additional unemployment. It can at least be said, however, that by comparison with schemes of relief work, insurance and similar plans do ensure that the bulk of the relief goes directly to those unemployed—only about nine or ten per cent of the funds disbursed by the British unemployment insurance scheme represent costs of administration. As against this, it is clear that the mere provision of monetary relief is not sufficient to maintain industrial capacity and prevent loss of morale. At various periods, it is true, official inquiries have been made which showed (on the basis of the examination of sample groups) that the percentage of persons claiming British unemployment benefit who could be described as "verging on the unemployable", or "whose acceptance by an employer would be doubtful", was very small indeed. This is, however, not as re-assuring as it sounds; for in these inquiries no account was taken of those who had fallen through the meshes of the insurance scheme into the public assistance net. The existence of efficient insurance or financial relief machinery does, it is to be feared, lull governments into a sense of false security; for, despite the setting-up of official training centres and junior instruction centres, and despite efforts by numerous voluntary agencies, this country makes less provision for physical and vocational training of the unemployed than many other countries (e.g. Italy and Germany) and has only recently begun to wake up to the fact.

5. *Leisure-time Activities*

This last point raises an issue of a more general character. What should be the state's attitude towards the leisure-time of workers? The progressive shortening of hours and the emergence of large-scale unemployment have made it necessary for governments to give serious consideration to this problem in the last few years. Broadly speaking, the liberal state confines itself to the encouragement, by financial and other means, of certain types of spare-time occupation; the only important case in which it goes beyond mere encouragement, (so far as those over school-age are concerned)[1] is where it makes the receipt of unemployment relief or public assistance conditional on attendance at a training camp or occupational centre. Thus in this country organized leisure activities are in the hands of business concerns or of voluntary agencies (including trade unions) for the most part; though local authorities have provided free libraries, art galleries, and museums and cheap opportunities of listening to concerts and lectures, or playing golf or tennis; but no one is compelled to make use of any of these facilities. It is worth noticing, however, that where the state or some local authority gives financial encouragement to any form of leisure-time activity, it exerts a fair measure of control over the form which activities receiving this subsidy shall take. Thus parliamentary control of B.B.C. policy, though not continuous, is shown when the B.B.C. charter (by virtue of which broadcasting is provided) comes up for renewal; detailed control of adult education classes receiving a state grant is exercised by the Board of Education and its inspectors; and, more recently, a National Advisory Council and a network of local committees have been set-up to see that government grants towards the improvement of physical fitness are spent in the most effective manner. Control, in these and other cases, takes the form of ensuring that the facilities provided reach a certain educational stan-

[1] In this country those under 18 can, if not fully employed, be required by the Minister of Labour to attend courses of instruction.

dard (either physically or mentally); that political propaganda is not subsidized; and sometimes also that a certain maximum cost per head is not exceeded.

The totalitarian state, of course, goes far beyond this. In Italy, Germany and the U.S.S.R. it is a matter of vital importance to the state how its constituent units spend their spare time; "their" spare time is, indeed, the state's time, in the sense that the method of its use must be such as to increase or maintain their efficiency as part of what its opponents call the state machine. Physical education, instead of merely being subsidized and encouraged, therefore, becomes compulsory and state-controlled. Other forms of leisure-time activity must also serve the same purpose of increasing efficiency —the music and lectures listened-to, the sculpture, paintings, plays and films looked-at, the newspapers and books read, must all play their part in leading to the more ready understanding and acceptance of the prevailing orthodoxy. State-controlled organizations such as the German "Strength through Joy" (Kraft durch Freude) and the Italian "National Workers' Leisure Time Institute" (Opera Nationale Dopolavoro) therefore constitute a logical development from the fundamental philosophy underlying the totalitarian state.

It is, however, no longer safe to assume that a hard-and-fast line can be drawn between totalitarian and liberal states in respect of their attitude towards the leisure-time of their citizens. In Belgium almost immediately after the War there was set up the Hainult Provincial Commission, charged with the co-ordination and provision of spare-time activities in a limited area; while in 1929 the co-operative movement in France (but not, it is true, the state) set up a "National Leisure-

Time Committee" (Comité National des Loisirs) with a comprehensive programme of activities, including the creation of centres of culture where local educative facilities were lacking, and the provision of facilities for physical education and travel. These are, of course, only beginnings, and it is even arguable that they bear little resemblance to totalitarian expedients; but they do suggest a tendency to look at leisure-time activities *as a whole*, which may prove to be a first step towards their ultimate active control.

FURTHER READING

In addition to some of the books listed in the last chapter (particularly *Unemployment: an International Problem* (1935) and the I.L.O., *International Survey of Social Services 1933* (2 vols. 1936)) the following may be mentioned. For Britain J. Cohen, *Insurance against Unemployment* (1931); R. C. Davison, *The Unemployed* (1929); M. B. Gilson, *Unemployment Insurance in Great Britain* (1931); Royal Commission on Unemployment Insurance, *Minutes of Evidence and Reports* (1931-32); and A. C. C. Hill, Jr., and I. Lubin, *The British Attack on Unemployment* (1934). A more recent work—T. S. Simey, *Principles of Social Administration* (1937)—stresses the dangers of undue centralization. Books which, emphasizing certain features of British unemployment, have a distinct bearing on the question of methods of relief, include S. P. B. Mais, *S.O.S. Talks on Unemployment* (1933); J. M. Williams, *Human Aspects of Unemployment and Relief* (1933); H. L. Beales and R. S. Lambert, *Memoirs of the Unemployed* (1934); J. Jewkes and A. Winterbottom, *Juvenile Unemployment* (1933); and V. A. Bell, *Junior Instruction Centres and their Future* (1934).

For other countries, two further I.L.O. publications may be found useful for reference—*Unemployment: Some International Aspects 1920-28* (1929); and *Bibliography of Unemployment 1920-29* (1930). For the United States, there are a number of monographs on the "poor law" in individual states, one important series being sponsored by the University of Chicago. There is no very satisfactory single work dealing with methods of relief throughout the United States during the recent depression, but M. Davis, *They Shall Not Want* (1937)—in which some comparison is made with conditions in Britain and Sweden—provides some useful material; it can be supplemented by articles in American journals of economics. The French system of relief is well described in G. Héreil, *Le Chômage en France* (1932). For Germany, O. Weigert, *Administration of Placement and Unemployment Insurance in Germany* (1934), still in large part applicable, can be supplemented by articles in the *International Labour Review*.

The best introduction to the subject of organized leisure-time is probably the I.L.O. Report, *Recreation and Education* (1936). E. Wernert, *L'art dans le Troisième Reich* (1936) is also well worth reading.

THE INTERNATIONAL LABOUR ORGANIZATION

AS we have seen, failure of governments to insist on high standards in respect of the treatment of labour is sometimes due to the fear that other countries will not follow their example, with the result that the international competing power of the country maintaining high standards will be impaired. If international agreement in these matters could be obtained, therefore, one of the factors at present inhibiting government action would be removed. An international conference on labour legislation was held as long ago as 1890; but the governments of the countries represented at that conference were unwilling to pledge themselves to take any definite action. Ten years later, however, an International Association for Labour Legislation was formed in Paris, and, as a result of its efforts, a conference was held in 1905 from which there emerged the famous Berne Convention of 1906. In order not to jeopardize the success of the venture, the subjects chosen for discussion were two on which a fair measure of agreement might be expected, and yet the urgency of which was likely to impress itself on the public mind. They were firstly, the prohibition of the industrial employment of women at night; and secondly, the prohibition of the manufacture and sale of matches made with white phosphorus. Of the fifteen states

represented, fourteen signed the first of these conventions; but as Japan refused to sign the second,
European countries interested in exporting matches
were reluctant to do so, and only six countries (in two
of which the prohibition was already in force) agreed
to sign the second convention. Not long afterwards,
however, several of the non-signatories were won round,
partly by the pressure of public opinion.

The possibility of successful action, and the practical
difficulties to be overcome, had both been demonstrated
by this pre-war experience; and when the threads were
taken up again after the War, there was every hope of
securing a substantial measure of international agreement on labour questions. Indeed, the Treaty of
Versailles set up a permanent organization for this very
purpose. In that treaty it was pointed out that peace
could only be based on social justice; that conditions of
labour existed involving such serious hardship and
injustice as to imperil peace; and that accordingly it
was appropriate for the League of Nations to take
special steps to eliminate these conditions. The application of nine "methods and principles for regulating
labour conditions" was declared to be of special
urgency. These were that labour should not be
regarded merely as an article of commerce; that workers
should be allowed to form associations for all lawful
purposes; that wages adequate to maintain a reasonable
standard of life should be paid; that the eight-hour day
or forty-eight hour week should be aimed at; that a
weekly twenty-four hour rest should be adopted; that
child labour should be abolished, and the hours of work
of young persons be restricted; that men and women
should receive equal pay for equal work; that the
equitable treatment of all workers in a country should

be secured; and that inspection—in which women should take part—should be employed to ensure the carrying-out of labour legislation.   At first sight it might appear that most of these reforms are now of merely academic interest; but a moment's consideration will show how far short of even this minimum programme the United States of America, for example, fell as recently as 1933; and America and, indeed, most countries still fall short of it in many respects.

The permanent organization which was created to facilitate international improvement of labour conditions consisted of a general conference of representatives of the members,[1] a governing body, and an international labour office.   Members send four representatives to the General Conference—two government spokesmen, a workers' and an employers' representative—and it is at this conference that all important decisions are taken.   The Governing Body is, in effect, a committee of the General Conference, which functions in the interval between the meetings of the Conference; it controls the International Labour Office, the main function of which is to collect and distribute information on labour problems, particularly those problems which the Conference is to discuss in the near future.   The research work undertaken by, or at the request of, the International Labour Office is of the greatest value not only to the Organization itself, but also to every one interested in post-war labour questions.

Once the Conference has shown itself in favour of some proposal (and due regard has been paid to the

[1] Membership of the League of Nations carries membership of this organization with it; certain non-members of the League have, however, joined, the United States being one.

effects of differences in climate, industrial organization and so on between one country and another) there remains the choice of the form the proposal should take —whether, that is to say, a recommendation or a draft convention is the more suitable form. Members undertake to submit both recommendations and draft conventions to their legislatures within a certain time, and to inform the Secretary-General of the action taken; but whereas the carrying-out of a recommendation leaves a good deal of latitude in the matter of the form the appropriate legislation shall take, the ratification of a convention is more like becoming a party to an international treaty, the undertaking thereby entered-into being explicit in character. Naturally, of course, members' representatives at the Conference have no power finally to accept any plan, except as a proposal.

What, then, have been the results achieved by this Organization? It is easy to point out that the number of ratifications obtained, and the importance of the subjects covered by these ratifications, are disappointing if measured by the standard of what, in 1918-19, it was hoped to achieve. There are two answers to this criticism, however. The first is that the non-fulfilment of the hopes of the immediate post-war years is not confined to international labour standards, but extends to all aspects of international action—including disarmament, peaceful settlement of disputes, and monetary and trade policy. A second answer lies in the fact that the success of the Organization is not to be measured solely by ratifications. Its influence in the education of public opinion (and hence of governments) in social questions, though gradual, is beginning to bear valuable fruit at the present time.

Further Reading

The best general survey of the International Labour Organization's work is contained in *The International Labour Organisation: the First Decade* (1931). This should be supplemented by the annual *Reports of the Director*, published since then; by F. G. Wilson, *Labor in the League System* (1934); and, of course, by the *International Labour Review*. G. Scelle *L'organisation Internationale du Travail et le B.I.T.* (1930) contains a good discussion of the legal problems involved. As an indication of early hopes, a series of essays published under the editorship of E. J. Solano, *Labour as an International Problem* (1920) is good. A useful Lecture by Professor Florence has been printed—P.S. Florence, *International Industrial Problems and the I.L.O.* (1937).

THE END

MADE AND PRINTED IN GREAT BRITAIN BY
EBENEZER BAYLIS AND SON, LTD., THE
TRINITY PRESS, WORCESTER, AND LONDON